THE
CHESAPEAKE BAY
Oyster
COOKBOOK

WHITEY SCHMIDT

"I think oysters are more beautiful than any religion . . . They not only forgive our unkindness to them; they justify it, they incite us to go on being perfectly horrid to them. Once they arrive at the supper table they seem to enter thoroughly into the spirit of the thing. There's nothing in Christianity or Buddhism that quite matches the sympathetic unselfishness of the oyster."

Hector Munro, The Matchmaker

Printed in the
United States of America

First Printing, Year 2003

ISBN 0-9613008-0-9

Library of Congress Catalog Number in publication data

© 2003 by Marian Hartnett Press
Box 88, Crisfield, Maryland 21817

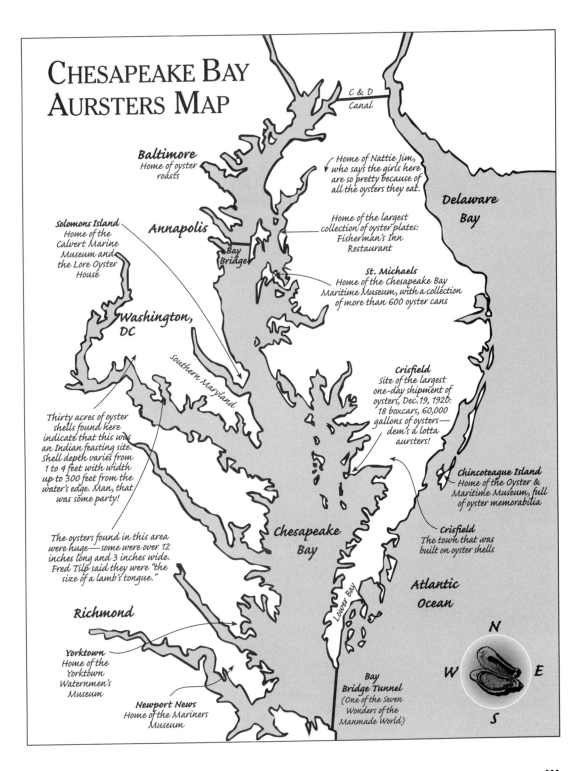

CHESAPEAKE BAY AURSTERS MAP

C & D Canal

Baltimore
Home of oyster roasts

Home of Nattie Jim, who says the girls here are so pretty because of all the oysters they eat.

Delaware Bay

Solomons Island
Home of the Calvert Marine Museum and the Lore Oyster House

Annapolis

Bay Bridge

Home of the largest collection of oyster plates: Fisherman's Inn Restaurant

St. Michaels
Home of the Chesapeake Bay Maritime Museum, with a collection of more than 600 oyster cans

Washington, DC

Southern Maryland

Crisfield
Site of the largest one-day shipment of oysters, Dec. 19, 1920: 18 boxcars, 60,000 gallons of oysters— dem's a lotta aursters!

Thirty acres of oyster shells found here indicate that this was an Indian feasting site. Shell depth varies from 1 to 4 feet with width up to 300 feet from the water's edge. Man, that was some party!

Chincoteague Island
Home of the Oyster & Maritime Museum, full of oyster memorabilia

Crisfield
The town that was built on oyster shells

The oysters found in this area were huge—some were over 12 inches long and 3 inches wide. Fred Tilp said they were "the size of a lamb's tongue."

Chesapeake Bay

Atlantic Ocean

Lower Bay

Richmond

Yorktown
Home of the Yorktown Watermen's Museum

Newport News
Home of the Mariners Museum

Bay Bridge Tunnel
(One of the Seven Wonders of the Manmade World)

N
W   E
S

CONTENTS

These oysters and crack knife were created by wildlife carver Walt Schmitz, Atlantic, Virginia.

vi

INTRODUCTION

When I was growing up on the Western Shore of the Chesapeake Bay, I remember hearing a lot about how great oysters were. When they weren't feasting on blue crabs, all the people in my neighborhood talked about the "R" months and how many oysters they'd eat once the season rolled around.

Pop Schmidt sure loved them. Whenever they were in season, I remember he'd steam, scald, barbecue, and slurp them by the dozen. But I wasn't convinced. To my juvenile eyes they just looked kinda . . . well, they didn't look like hamburgers.

So it was with a little trepidation that I finally took Pop up on his offer and tried my first fried oyster (I was a teenager by then, if you can believe it). But as soon as I tasted it, I was hooked. There was just something unique about the flavor—or flavors. Already a huge fan of the Bay's other catches—rockfish, croaker, and, of course, blue crabs—I found this new taste something more complex and suitable to my "maturing palate."

I recall the taste well, and have recreated it countless times since here in my Crisfield kitchen (known as the Crab Lab to my friends, but also used for oyster research). First, there was the taste of the sea: briny, meaty, dramatic. That was followed by a slight mineral richness, which was then followed by a lingering, pleasant aftertaste that was even smoother than the flavor of the oyster itself.

I'd like to think that Pop would be proud of how seriously I take oysters today. Since my first dalliance with the oyster, I've learned to appreciate it for more than its flavor, and I'm not alone. Here in Chesapeake country, the oyster is not so much a menu item as it is a legitimate subculture all its own.

We write poems about oysters; we venerate the watermen who harvest oysters. We hold oyster roasts and oyster festivals that can draw tens of thousands of devotees in a single weekend. Personally, I spend countless hours standing around the Crab Lab with friends, popping oysters (the local Chincoteague salts are my favorite), cracking beers, and whipping up old recipes—and some brand new ones—while we slurp oysters and talk about everything from wine to women and . . . well, wine and women.

In short, we love our oysters. And why shouldn't we? Oystering on the Chesapeake goes back many, many generations. Bivalves are in our blood. All around the Bay, there are families today who are still oystering and can trace their oystering lineage back to the turn of the last century—indeed the golden era for oysters on the Chesapeake.

Rather than the dozen or so skipjack fishing boats we have plying the Bay today for oysters, there were literally thousands doing so in the early 1900s. Their captains—a motley assortment of profiteers and pirates—came from all over the world to cash in on the Bay's "oyster rush" the same way prospectors swarmed San Francisco in 1849.

I can think back and imagine what that must have been like. Those beautiful wooden sailboats chasing after countless oysters on the Chesapeake, the characters, stories, and skirting of the law. The rum. The profits. The oysters! I don't know. Maybe I'm just an old romantic. Maybe I was born in the wrong era. But I doubt it. Because just up the road from my house here in Crisfield, I still know a guy who'll sell me a bushel for less than fifty bucks.

Enjoy.

Whitey Schmidt

A CHESAPEAKE AURSTERS DICTIONARY

Asian oysters—Asian oysters look good and taste so much like our own native oysters that even experts can't tell them apart.

aursters—Oysters on the Chesapeake Bay contain an abundance of minerals and vitamins, including iron, copper, iodine, calcium, phosphorus, and vitamins A, B, C, D, and E.

Bayside oysters—Oysters grown Bayside of the Chesapeake.

box—Dead oyster: "We caught 6 bushel of oysters today. 'Bout half was *boxes*."

bugeye—A double-ended sailing workboat with two triangular sales and a jib. It's used for oyster dredging on the Bay.

bunch oysters—Oysters that grow in clusters.

buy boat—A boat used in the purchase of oysters at the oyster grounds. Operators of buy boats purchase oysters from tongers and then rush them to market.

Chesapeake stabber—A favorite oyster knife of the Chesapeake watermen.

Chincoteague oysters—Or Chincoteague salts. An oyster grown around Chincoteague Island, Virginia.

cracker—One who opens oysters by breaking the shell with a hammer; also called "billing."

Crisfield murlin—Crisfield, Maryland, a town built on oyster shells.

culling—Separating smaller oysters from larger ones; *grading*.

culls—Oysters that are too small to be harvested.

cultch—The substrate to which spat attaches itself. Bits and pieces of oyster shell are the most common cultch.

culture—Growing oysters. See also *ground culture, raft culture, rack culture, stake culture*.

Dooley's Prong—A tributary of Piccowaxen Creek off the Potomac River. It is the site of the largest Indian oyster-shell field on the Bay.

ersters—Eastern Shore slang for oysters.

grading—See *culling*.

ground culture—Farming oysters on the bottom of the Bay.

half sacker—Someone who steals oysters from oyster beds.

J.O. Spice—Popular Chesapeake seasoning.

Old Bay—Popular Chesapeake seasoning.

oyster cans—Oysters were shipped throughout the American Midwest in cans packed in wooden cases. Today they are valued by antique collectors.

oyster crackers—A popular cracker served with oyster stews.

oyster drudge (dredge)—A powerful work barge used to harvest, transport, culture, or plant oysters.

oyster knife—See *Chesapeake stabber.*

oyster liquor—The juices found in freshly shucked oysters.

oyster shooter—A popular bar drink made with beer or vodka. See Chapter 5.

peacemaker—See *Oyster Loaf with Blue Cheese Crumble,* page 75.

pea crab—A tiny crab that lives in a live oyster.

rack culture—Farming oysters in fixed racks off the bottom of the Bay.

raft culture—Farming oysters suspended from floats.

rock salt—Used for keeping oysters from spilling contents when they are baked in a hot oven.

seaside oysters—Oysters grown off the Atlantic side of the Virginia coast.

seed—Young oysters.

shucker—One who opens oysters and removes the meat from the shell. A good shucker can shuck 12 to 14 gallons a day.

skimming table—A shallow, perforated, stainless steel tray for washing, inspecting, and grading shucked oysters.

skipjack—A popular type of sailboat designed for dredging oysters.

spat—A common term in oyster farming that refers to the stage in which free-swimming larvae settle on the bottom, attaching themselves to *cultch.*

stake culture—Farming oysters by attaching seed to small stakes about 10 inches above the mud.

tongs—A tool used to manually gather oysters in deep water. Tongs were developed in the 17th century and are shaped like big scissors with rakes at the ends of the "blades."

waterman—One who makes a living harvesting Chesapeake oysters, crabs, and fish.

Photograph by Marion E. Warren

3

TIPS FOR BUYING OYSTERS

There's an old belief traced back to the Middle Ages that oysters are good to eat only in the "R" months, September through April. In fact, oysters are good—as well as safe—to eat in any month of the year. The "R-less" months are spawning months for oysters, though, and their beds are best not disturbed then.

All oysters are harvested, processed, and shipped under rigid state and federal health requirements to ensure the highest possible quality. To confirm an oysters freshness, give the shell a tap. A truly fresh one will close its shell up tight.

More tips:

- Oysters in the shell are usually sold by the dozen, the bushel, or the box. The box or bushel contain approximately 200 oysters. Two dozen oysters in the shell equal about 1 pint of shucked oysters.

- Fresh shucked oysters can be purchased by the pint or quart. Look for clear—not cloudy—liquid surrounding the oysters. One pint equals six servings. "Selects" is the name given the largest of the shucked oysters; "standard" is the term used for average size oysters; "stewing" oysters are small.

- The color of oysters may vary depending on what it has eaten or because a rapid change in temperature. A freshly shucked oyster could be gray, creamy, brownish, pale yellow, red, green, or a combination of these colors. They are quite safe to eat regardless of color.

- Live oysters in the shell last 7 to 10 days on ice or in the refrigerator; refrigerate shucked oysters up to a week.

PEARLS OF KNOWLEDGE

- Oysters are high in protein and minerals and low in fat. They contain zinc and potassium as well as vitamins A, B (thiamin, riboflavin, niacin, B-12, pantothenic acid), C, D, and G.

- A quart of oysters has more protein than a quart of milk. Six ounces contain more than half the minimum daily requirement of iron and copper, half the iodine, and one-tenth the recommended amount of protein, calcium, magnesium, and phosphorus.

- Three ounces of oysters contain only 72 calories.

- The flesh of the oyster is not the mollusk's only gem. Sometimes you'll find inside the oyster a tiny pea crab. This minute crustacean has become known as the oyster crab. it's considered by many to be a delicacy.

WHITEY'S OYSTER ROASTS

The ingredients for an oyster roast are simple: a roaring fire, a bushel or two of fresh oysters, melted butter, lemon wedges, cocktail sauce, ice-cold beer, white wine or champagne, and plenty of people.

A bushel of oysters will generally serve 15 to 20 people. Clean the oyster shells under cold running water with a brush (wear an apron and heavy gloves) to remove all mud and debris.

Build a fire and let it burn for about an hour, or until the coals are very hot. Place a metal plate or grill over the fire. When the fire has burned down to a bed of hot coals, place a quarter-bushel of oysters on the hot metal plate.

Cover the oysters completely with wet burlap sacks. The heat hitting the wet sacks produces steam, which cooks the oysters. In 5 to 10 minutes, the oyster shells will start popping open. Remove the steaming oysters from the fire and open the shells with an oyster knife.

Cook the remaining oysters in the same manner. Serve them with melted butter, lemon wedges, or cocktail sauce.

If you can't build an open fire, or don't want to, you can roast the oysters on a barbecue grill—you just can't cook as many at one time. Place the oysters on a hot grill and cover them with a wet towel.

Aw, Shucks

Tips from Around the Bay on Opening Fresh Oysters That Don't Want to Be Opened

Opening an oyster can be a trying—even a blood-letting—experience, but it needn't be if you follow these tips (although it likely will be at first, but you'll get better with experience).

You can, of course, pay someone to shuck your fresh oysters. As you can see by the sign at right, there are experts out there willing to shuck a dozen for three dollars. But in my universe, that's half a bottle of drinkable wine. So it's worth it to learn your own method. You can even take the class I took from the Maryland Watermen's Association (see my certificate below) to learn how the pros do it.

But it seems everyone has his particular way of separating two halves of the bivalves. Here we take a look at some of my favorites . . .

[Note: It's important to keep the proper equipment on hand to shuck your oysters. Use an actual oyster knife (short, strong, dull blade and fat handle). Wear heavy work gloves to prevent the knife from poking your hand. And don't forget to scrub the oysters beforehand, using a stiff-bristled vegetable brush under cold running water. Good luck!]

Maryland Watermen's Association
Oyster Shucking Demonstration conducted at
The Annual Chesapeake Appreciation Days

"King Oyster"

This certifies that

WHITEY SCHMIDT

has this day successfully completed the INTRODUCTORY SEMINAR in
BASIC OYSTER SHUCKING TECHNIQUES
conducted under the supervision of the MARYLAND WATERMEN's
ASSOCIATION at Sandy Point State Park, Annapolis, Maryland.

Given this Day ___ 10/30/88 ___

under my Hand and Seal: ___ Ken Bunny ___

6

TIPS AND TRICKS

"Why, then the World's mine oyster which I
with sword will open." —BILL SHAKESPEARE,
THE MERRY WIVES OF WINDSOR

"In your left hand, near its wide end and with
the flat shell up, wiggle the oyster-knife point.
Where the top and bottom shells come
together, enter the knife at 5 o'clock and go to
9 o'clock. Cut the muscle from the top shell,
remove the top shell and cut the muscle from
the bottom one, being careful to preserve the
natural juice, the liquor, of the oyster."

—BETTY DUTY, MARYLAND WATERMEN'S ASSOCIATION

"I let my wife Mary do it. She's much better.
And quicker." —VINCE LUPO

"Put 'em in the microwave and nuke 'em till
they open. That always works."

—CRISFIELD BILL

"Man, I use a church key. Insert the pointed end
into the hinge and pop it open that way."

—RON WHITE

"My system if foolproof. I wear my heavy boots
and wedge a large screwdriver into the hinge
end and step down on the handle. Opens them
every time." —BRIGGS WHITE

SEMI-OFFICIAL "TECHNIQUES"

Billing: This is even simpler than Briggs'
method. You just take a hammer and knock off
about half an inch of the shell at the thin end.
This provides an opening for the oyster knife.
Voilà. Another name for this method is the Old
Chincoteague Breaker Method.

Hinge Method: Some of the world's fastest
shuckers use this method, which involves going
in at the hinge, finding the pressure point and
popping the shell open. This can be a great way
for beginners to start off, too. My old friend
Ron White is an example of a hinge popper.

The Traditional Method: This is basically the
method described by Betty Duty. Some call it
the 5-to-9 method. I call it the Bay Stabber
Method. Usually I'm the one who gets stabbed,
not the oyster.

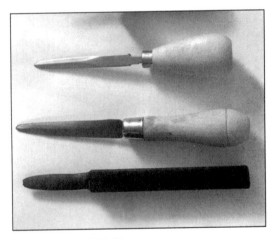

Top: Chesapeak Stabber

Middle: Gulf Coaster

Bottom: Crack knife

ACKNOWLEDGMENTS

This cookbook has been made possible through the efforts of the following groups and individuals.

Traugott Schmidt
TAB Distributing Co.
Sue Knopf, Graffolio
Denise McDonald, cover
   design
Robin Quinn
Pat Piper
Bill and Gracie Schmidt
Judy Hopkins
Talbot Kitchens
Elise Reed
Janet Murray
Bill Murray
Jay Livingston
Melissa Livingston

Chesapeake Bay Maritime
   Museum
Calvert Marine Museum
Oyster & Maritime
   Museum, Chincoteague,
   VA
Mariners Museum
Watermen's Museum
Oyster Recovery
   Partnership, Annapolis,
   MD
Graham Bruce
Henry Wagner
Ron White
Briggs White
Taylor Odend'hal

Gloria Odend'hal
José Garham
Southern Connection
   Seafood
United States Post Office,
   Crisfield, MD
Barb and Dan Kuehler
Vince Lupo
Matt Schmidt
Larry Antonik
Ruth and Rob McBrayer
Wood-A-Drift Art Shop
Peanutts Wise
Mary Riley
Metompkin Bay Oyster Co.

SELECTED PHOTOGRAPH CREDITS

A. Aubrey Bodine, © Jennifer B. Bodine, courtesy of AAubreyBodine.com, 202, 203, 205, 206, 207

Sam Gunby, 31

Bryan Hatchett, 30, 55, 66, 197

Vince Lupo, front and back covers, iv, v, vi, 11, 15, 37, 41, 46, 47, 61, 86, 89, 95, 98, 106, 108, 109, 111, 164, 166, 167, 168, 170, 175, 198, 209, 211, 214, 220, 222, 223, 288, and color insert photos

The Maritime Museum, Newport News, Virginia, 192, 193, 199, 204, 208

Pat Piper, 91, 218

Scorchy Tawes, 145

Marion E. Warren, 3, 65, 91, 187, 189, 190, 191, 218

Ron White, 210

SELECTED ARTWORK CREDITS

Betsy Kehne illustration, 71

Tighty Mister Collections photographs and post cards, 143, 144, 146, 147, 148, 152, 153

John Ritter painting, 20

Ed Spinney illustration, 23

Dale Tolly painting, 114

Mary Lou Troutman painting, 27

CRAB LAB TASTE TESTERS

All of the recipes in this book have been tested at least once—some many times. A special thanks goes to these Crab Lab Taste Testers, who have spent countless hours testing and tasting recipes and commenting on flavor and appearance. Thank you all for your enthusiasm for oyster cookery. As I always say, "It's a tough job, but someone has to do it."

Bill Schmidt
Gracie Schmidt
Matt Schmidt
Dean Gore
Tom Vernon
Jay Livingston
Melissa Livingston
Raymond McAlwee
Damien Heaney
Pat Piper
Bryan Hatchett
Vince Lupo
Bo Herrman
Ray Durham
Traugott Schmidt

Barb Kuebler
Dan Kuebler
Ron White
Briggs White
Susan Wills
Carol Hammond
Bob Hammond
Susan Glaser
Greg Berczansky
Chuck Fourhman
Steven Lenosky
Erik Turner
Mike Brodie
Scott Moore
Steve Farnsworth

Todd Mullen
Shai Ivgi
Sandra Cogswell
Russell Dashiell, Jr.
Jo Ann Dashiell
Jim Ritz
Peggy Gore
Gloria Odend'hal
Ruth McBrayer
Rob McBrayer
Mary Riley
Sherry White
Margaret Hatchett
Eyvonne Marceau
Barbara Berti

Linda Meyer
José Garnham
Barb Garnham
Taylor Odend'hal
Angie Machotto
Barbara Lausche
Terry Pehan
Connie Pehan
Pam Cline
John Cline
The gang at Setter's Point

AURSTER PANTRY

The Chesapeake Bay region has distinctive ingredients, spices, herbs, seasonings that are used in certain ways or combinations that give "Chesapeake Cuisine" its unique characteristics. Here are a few of my favorites:

Old Bay seasoning—Old Bay is a blend of herbs and spices that is used around Bay Country kitchens.

J.O. Spice—People ask me all the time about the secret to Chesapeake Bay cooking. The secret is in the seasonings. Seasoning doesn't mean it's hot and spicy, but that it's a perfect balance of spices and herbs in just the right proportions to complement the dish that it's used in.

Tabasco® sauce—Tabasco is an extremely hot spicy sauce made from red peppers. Tabasco is used as a condiment and for enlivening oyster dishes. I love to put a few drops on a freshly shucked oyster.

Parmigiano-Reggiano cheese—This hard, dry cheese is made from skimmed cow's milk. It has a hard, pale-golden rind, a straw-colored interior, and a rich, sharp flavor. I look for the words "Parmigiano-Reggiano" stamped on the rind. In the Crab Lab kitchen, it's the best of the best.

Lemons—The lemon has a multitude of culinary uses for dishes from sweet to savory. We always keep a dozen in the Crab Lab. You should, too!

Beer—Beer and oysters go together just like salt goes with French fries. In Chesapeake Country we have one rule—drink the one you like.

Wine—Same rule as beer. I love a buttery chardonnay to drink along with freshly shucked oysters.

Rock salt—Rock salt has a grayish cast because it is not as refined as other salts. It comes in chunky crystals and is used primarily as a bed on which to serve baked oysters.

CHAPTER 1
Oyster Art
& Appetizers

OYSTER-CHEESE APPETIZERS

Port wine cheddar is a popular coldpack cheese flavored with domestic port. For some reason it always makes me want to light the fireplace, set out some candles, and open a bottle of red wine.

    1   **pint oysters and liquor**
    8   **ounces port wine cheese**
   24   **sesame crackers**

Drain oysters and discard liquor. Place oysters in a single layer in a well-greased baking dish. Dot them with cheese. Bake at 350°F for 15 to 20 minutes or until edges of oysters curl and cheese melts. Remove each cheese-topped oyster from the baking dish with a fork and place on a sesame cracker.

Makes approximately 24 appetizers.

There's something about oyster advertisements that warms my heart. They might not be Picassos, but some of the signs show truly fine artwork, like this Troutly broadside by "Wm. P. Ketterer of 919 Windsor St., Reading, Pa."

GOODSELL ALLEY DEVILED OYSTERS

Like many traditional Chesapeake dishes, this simple deviled oyster bake is a terrific flavor showcase for the primary ingredient: fresh Bay oysters.

24	oysters in shells
1	tablespoon butter
2	tablespoons all-purpose flour
½	pint light cream
2	egg yolks
1	tablespoon minced celery
1	tablespoon minced fresh parsley
1	teaspoon minced fresh thyme
1	teaspoon dried mace
	salt and pepper
½	cup fresh bread crumbs
	butter

Shuck, drain, and chop the oysters, reserving the deep shells and discarding the oyster liquor. Melt 1 teaspoon butter over low heat and whisk in flour until smooth. Add cream and bring to a boil. Remove from heat and add egg yolks, celery, parsley, thyme, mace, and salt and pepper to taste. Butter insides of clean oyster shells and fill with the oyster mixture. Sprinkle with bread crumbs, dot with more butter, and bake at 425°F until golden brown, 15 to 20 minutes.

Serves 6.

I photographed this oyster sign at the Chesapeake Bay Maritime Museum in St. Michaels, Maryland. The new oyster exhibit there is not to be missed. The J.M. Clayton Co. on Cambridge Creek (Cambridge, Maryland) no longer deals in oysters, but it's still one of my favorite places to go for Maryland crabmeat.

Eat for Health's Sake
CHOICE CHESAPEAKE
EPICURE QUALITY BRAND
OYSTERS
PACKED AND GUARANTEED BY
J.M. CLAYTON CO.
CAMBRIDGE MD.

PLUM TREE OYSTERS & FRENCH BREAD

 *You can't get much quicker or easier than this fresh and light lunch. It's important to have good bread—like a San Francisco-style sourdough—so you can sop up all the wonderful juices.*

1   **pint oysters and liquor**
⅓   **cup butter**
1   **tablespoon chopped fresh parsley**
3   **teaspoons minced garlic**
1   **loaf French bread, sliced and toasted**

Drain oysters and reserve 6 tablespoons of the liquor. Melt butter in a medium skillet. Add parsley, oyster liquor, and garlic. Cook 2 minutes. Add oysters and cook 3 to 5 minutes or until edges curl. Serve in individual dishes with French bread.

Serves 4 to 6.

I noticed the sign. I snapped the photo. I opened the door to the market. I purchased one pint of clams, one pint of oysters. I topped my lunch off with a bowl of steaming, singing chowder and I thought about you. Well, maybe I didn't think about you.

LOWER MARLBORO OYSTERS WITH ROASTED GARLIC

Garlic adds unmistakable character to freshly shucked oysters and imparts taste bud-tingling flavor, especially when served with crusty bread and washed down with a frothy mug of beer.

2 **large heads garlic**
2 **sticks unsalted butter**
½ **cup olive oil**
36 **oysters in shells**
2 **cups heavy cream**
   salt and pepper

Separate the cloves of garlic and place them, unpeeled, in a small oven-proof dish. Cut the butter into pieces and place them on top of the garlic. Drizzle with the olive oil, cover the dish with foil, and bake at 250°F for 2 to 3 hours or until the garlic is very soft. When they're cool, carefully peel the skins from the garlic cloves, discard the skins, and set the cloves aside. Refrigerate the garlic butter mixture.

Scrub oyster shells under cold running water. Shuck and drain the oysters and reserve the liquor and deep shells. Combine the liquor and cream and simmer until it reduces to 1½ cups. Season with salt and pepper.

To assemble: Preheat the oven to 425°F. Place oysters and garlic cloves in the oyster shells and place on a baking sheet. Pour in enough of the hot cream mixture to cover. Bake for 15 minutes and serve hot, topped with small pieces of the refrigerated garlic butter.

Serves 12.

Photograph by Vince Lupo.

"The eldest oyster looked at him/But never a word he said./The eldest oyster winked his eye, and shook his heavy head—/Meaning to say he did not choose to leave the oyster bed."
—Lewis Carroll,
"The Walrus and the Carpenter"

OYSTER COCKTAIL

The sauce for this dish will be sure to please certain palates. Some purists demand that their oysters be served undefiled by any other flavors, whether from seasonings, herbs, or condiments, so always ask before serving.

    12 oysters in shells
     1 teaspoon lemon juice
     2 teaspoons tomato ketchup
        dash of Tabasco sauce
    ½   teaspoon salt
    ½   teaspoon sugar

Shuck and drain the oysters, discarding shells and oyster liquor. Chill the oysters. Mix lemon juice, ketchup, Tabasco sauce, salt and sugar. Chill. To serve, divide oysters between 2 cocktail or sherbet glasses. Pour dressing over oysters and serve immediately.

Serves 2.

One of my favorite seafood markets is Kool Ice and Seafood in Cambridge, Maryland. This is one of those spots where the local watermen unload their daily catch. (And from the looks of this sign, it's where hunters store their fresh venison, too.)

POINT LOOKOUT OYSTER POINTS

Point Lookout in Southern Maryland is located at the confluence of the Chesapeake Bay and the Potomac River and has always been one of my favorite haunts. The area has plenty to offer, and when it offered me a bushel of fresh local oysters, this recipe was the result.

1	pint oysters and liquor
½	pound mushrooms, sliced
3	tablespoons butter
3	tablespoons all-purpose flour
1	cup milk
½	teaspoon salt
¼	teaspoon celery salt
	freshly ground black pepper to taste
1	teaspoon lemon juice
12	toast points (6 slices of toast cut in half)
	fresh parsley

Drain oysters, discarding oyster liquor, and set aside. In a saucepan sauté mushrooms in butter until tender, blend in flour, and cook until bubbly. Gradually add milk and cook until smooth and thickened, stirring constantly. Add salt, celery salt, pepper, lemon juice, and oysters. Cook over medium-low heat until edges of oysters start to curl (about 5 minutes), stirring occasionally. Serve over toast points and garnish with parsley.

"We Decide," a citizens group on the lower Eastern Shore of Virginia, held a meeting to discuss issues concerning the future of the Shore. Can you think of a better way to boost attendance?

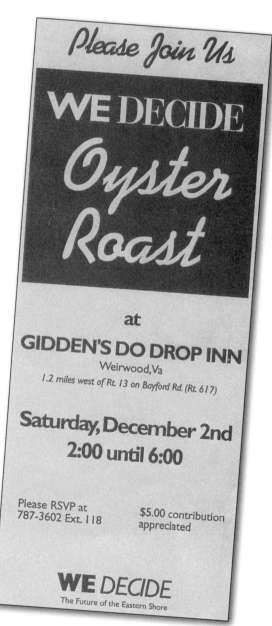

Please Join Us

WE DECIDE
Oyster Roast

at
GIDDEN'S DO DROP INN
Weirwood, Va
1.2 miles west of Rt. 13 on Bayford Rd. (Rt. 617)

Saturday, December 2nd
2:00 until 6:00

Please RSVP at
787-3602 Ext. 118

$5.00 contribution
appreciated

WE DECIDE
The Future of the Eastern Shore

Oysters-in-a-Biscuit

Maryland beaten biscuits have been around for ages and reflect the days when the first sound heard in the morning was the whack-whack of dough being repeatedly beaten with a rolling pin. After trying this recipe, the only sound you'll hear will be guests asking, "Are there any left?"

1	**quart oysters and liquor**
24	**2-inch beaten biscuits dinner rolls**
1	**stick butter, softened**
2	**teaspoons seafood seasoning**
	paprika

Drain oysters, pat them dry, and discard oyster liquor. Split rolls in half and hollow out centers. Thoroughly mix butter and seafood seasoning. Spread the mixture liberally on the rolls. Place 1 oyster on each half roll and sprinkle paprika on top. Broil until edges of oysters curl, about 4 to 5 minutes. Serve hot.

Makes 48 appetizers.

Hampton, Virginia's scenic harbor is a great place to visit and explore. One of my favorite places is the Oyster Alley bar in the Radisson Hotel. I love to sit there on the waterfront, slurp a dozen raw oysters, and drink a cold beer or two (sometimes three, but never more than ten).

SeaQuest Broiled Oysters with Crab

 A delicate topping of lump crabmeat and grated Parmesan livens up this dish. Try it and become a hero to your guests!

24	oysters in shells
½	teaspoon lemon juice
2	tablespoons chopped green onions
½	teaspoon minced fresh parsley
½	cup lump crabmeat
½	cup rolled cracker crumbs
2	tablespoons butter
2	tablespoons grated Parmigiano-Reggiano cheese

Scrub oyster shells under cold running water. Shuck oysters, remove them from shells, drain, then return them to their deep shells. Discard oyster liquor. Sauté the green onions and parsley in butter. Remove from the heat and mix in the cracker crumbs. Place a few drops of lemon juice on each oyster, cover with the crumb mixture, and place the oysters under the broiler for about 2 minutes. Remove and distribute the crabmeat over the oysters. Sprinkle tops with Parmigiano-Reggiano cheese and return to the broiler for 5 minutes.

Serves 4.

Collecting oyster plates and cans is a well-established hobby, but the same cannot be said of other oyster-related items. All throughout the oyster industry you'll find artifacts like tongs, rakes, bushel baskets and signs, many with great oyster art. I tend to purchase them with compulsive abandon.

WHITEHAVEN BROILED OYSTERS

Some say that oysters are an aphrodisiac, more powerful and potent than powdered rhino horns. It is a known fact that Casanova downed 50 or more salty ones before heading out for each evening's conquest. It only takes me a dozen.

36 oysters in shells
2 tablespoons lemon juice
   cayenne pepper to taste
1 stick butter
¼ cup all-purpose flour
1½ cups dry white wine
½ cup heavy cream
   salt and freshly ground black pepper
   dash of thyme
   grated Parmigiano-Reggiano cheese

Scrub oyster shells under cold, running water. Shuck and drain oysters, discarding oyster liquor and reserving deep shells. Place drained oysters in shells and sprinkle with the lemon juice and cayenne pepper. In a small saucepan, melt the butter and add the flour. Stir until the roux is smooth. Then blend in the wine, cream, salt, pepper, and thyme. Bring the sauce to a boil, then spoon this mixture over the oysters. Sprinkle each oyster with a little Parmigiano-Reggiano cheese. Broil 4 to 5 minutes.

Makes 36 appetizers.

Artist John Ritter explains: Skipjacks dredging for oysters on the Chesapeake Bay remain a common sight in the winter months and are easily recognizable by their raked masts and wide triangular sails. The defining characteristic of the skipjack, however, was the construction of the hull, not the sail plan. On this basis, the 50-foot Sallie Bramble, *pictured below was technically not a skipjack; she was a one-masted round-stern log-hulled bugeye built in Whitehaven, Maryland, on the Wicomico River in 1890. In this scene the brisk breeze required that its sail be shortened, or reefed.*

Painting by John Ritter.

Oysters on the Half-Shell

Oyster lovers who visit my Crisfield kitchen, the Crab Lab, can attest to one thing: the oysters are always ice-cold. We gather around the butcher block, oyster knives in hand, and attack piles of Chesapeake oysters just waiting to be shucked. This recipe is good if you're looking to impress someone special.

12	oysters in shells
5	cups crushed ice
1	lemon
	freshly cracked black pepper
	wine vinegar

COCKTAIL SAUCE

1	cup chili sauce
2	tablespoons prepared horseradish
2	tablespoons lemon juice
2	tablespoons finely chopped celery

Scrub oyster shells under cold running water. Just before serving, shuck them and strain the liquor that spills from each shell into a clean bowl. Arrange the oysters in their deep shells on a bed of ice and pour the strained liquor over them. Serve with a wedge of lemon, a bit of cracked pepper, and a splash of vinegar or cocktail sauce.

Cocktail Sauce: Mix all ingredients. Chill if not using immediately.

Serves 2.

I spotted this oyster art on the wall of an antiques shop in Easton, Maryland. It's memorabilia like this that keeps me from building a retirement fund. But then again, who's in a hurry to retire from writing oyster cookbooks?

SHIPS CABIN OYSTERS BINGO

The Ships Cabin is located on Ocean View Avenue in Norfolk, Virginia. It's no ordinary seafood house. This recipe, taken from their menu, will attest to the fact that the Ships Cabin is one of the best 100 restaurants in America.

  6   **oysters in shells**
  1   **tablespoon clarified butter**
  1   **tablespoon all-purpose flour plus additional for dredging**
  1   **ounce dry white wine**
  1   **teaspoon minced shallots**
  1   **teaspoon chopped fresh parsley a few drops of lemon juice salt and pepper**

Shuck the oysters, reserving the deep shells and straining the liquor that spills from each shell into a clean bowl. Put the shells in a 200°F oven to keep warm. Heat the butter in a sauté pan. Lightly flour the oysters and sauté until golden brown. Remove them from the pan and place them on the heated shells. Make a roux by adding 1 tablespoon of flour to the butter in the pan; add shallots, wine, reserved oyster liquor, and lemon juice. Heat until the sauce thickens. Season to taste with salt and pepper. Pour the sauce over the oysters and serve immediately.

Serves 1.

If you want to adopt an oyster, call the Oyster Recovery Partnership in Annapolis. (I like to adopt them by the dozen.) Did you know that oysters generally grow at the rate of about one inch per year and usually enter the market when they're three to five years old?

KING CARTER BROILED OYSTERS WITH BACON

It's hard to imagine party food in Bay country without thinking of broiled oysters. This recipe serves four, but can easily be doubled, tripled or quadrupled to feed more. When friends stop by, I just keep making these in batches, and they just keep disappearing (the oysters, that is).

24 oysters in shells
3 garlic cloves, minced
½ cup ketchup
   Tabasco sauce
6 slices bacon cut into 24 pieces

Shuck the oysters, discarding the oyster liquor and reserving the deep shells. Cut the bacon into 1-inch squares. Place the oysters in their deep shells and cover each with garlic and a piece of bacon. Top each with a little ketchup and a dash of Tabasco sauce. Broil until the bacon is crisp.

Serves 4.

Artist Ed Spinney explains that composing an interesting pen-and-ink is akin to developing an interesting short story. It begins with a solid concept of setting, light, time and place. The place for this drawing is Smith Point, Virginia. Thanks, Ed. It's beautiful.

Drawing by Ed Spinney.

BALTIMORE BROIL

Quick and delicious comfort foods are always great. I love cooking with the basics, such as these big white mushrooms, which are raised so close to the Bay shores around here that I can hear them growing at night. Or is that just a hangover from all the oyster liquor?

24   oysters in shells
24   large white mushrooms
4   tablespoons butter, melted
    salt and pepper
1   teaspoon dried rosemary
4   slices lean bacon, diced
4   slices buttered toast
    watercress

Shuck the oysters, reserving the deep shells and discarding the top shells and liquor. Set aside.

Remove the mushroom stems and discard. Dip the caps in melted butter and arrange them (tops up) on a rack in a shallow baking dish. Broil for 4 minutes. Remove them from the broiler and season with salt and pepper. Turn the caps over and sprinkle lightly with rosemary. Place an oyster in the hollow of each mushroom cap, cover with diced bacon, and return to the broiler. Broil for 3 minutes or until the bacon is golden brown. Serve piping hot on buttered toast garnished with watercress.

Serves 4.

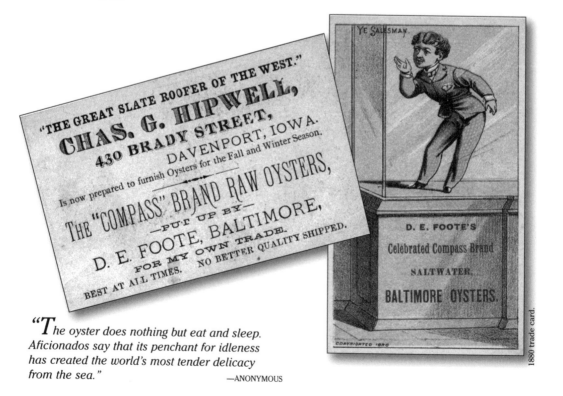

"THE GREAT SLATE ROOFER OF THE WEST."
CHAS. G. HIPWELL,
430 BRADY STREET,
DAVENPORT, IOWA.
Is now prepared to furnish Oysters for the Fall and Winter Season.
THE "COMPASS" BRAND RAW OYSTERS,
—PUT UP BY—
D. E. FOOTE, BALTIMORE,
FOR MY OWN TRADE.
BEST AT ALL TIMES. NO BETTER QUALITY SHIPPED.

YE SALESMAN.

D. E. FOOTE'S
Celebrated Compass Brand
SALTWATER,
BALTIMORE OYSTERS.

COPYRIGHTED 1880

1880 trade card.

"The oyster does nothing but eat and sleep. Aficionados say that its penchant for idleness has created the world's most tender delicacy from the sea." —ANONYMOUS

CHARM CITY OYSTER RAREBIT

Welsh rabbit, also known as Welsh rarebit, is usually just melted cheddar cheese, ale, and sometimes an egg, served on toast. Here's a Bay-flavored variation. It reminds me of a joke, which I first read in a Jonathan Bartlett cookbook: God in Heaven gets so annoyed with the rabble-rousing of his Welsh souls that he sends Peter outside the Heavenly gates and instructs him to yell: "Come git yer roast cheese!" When all the Welshmen have stormed out in pursuit of their favorite snack, Peter slams the gates shut.

1	**pint oysters and liquor**
2	**tablespoons butter**
¼	**pound Gruyère cheese**
	salt
	dash of cayenne pepper
	half-and-half
2	**egg yolks, beaten**
1	**teaspoon Worcestershire sauce**
4	**slices buttered toast cut in triangles**
	paprika

Cook the oysters in their liquor until plump. Drain the oysters and keep them warm. Reserve the liquor.

Boil water in the bottom of a double boiler. Add the butter, Gruyère cheese, ½ teaspoon salt, and cayenne pepper to the top of the double boiler: . Place the top of the double boiler over the boiling water. Add enough half-and-half to the reserved oyster liquor to make 1 cup. Add this mixture to the double boiler along with the egg yolks, stirring constantly. Continue to cook and beat until the sauce thickens. Add the warm oysters and season with more salt to taste. Add the Worcestershire sauce. Serve on toast garnished with a sprinkling of paprika.

Serves 4.

Freeman and Shaw—Horseshoe Brand oyster art. This piece is called "The Child." You can tell by the look on her face that she ate the last oyster.

CAPTAIN FAUNCE OYSTER DELIGHT

 Webster's definition of sauce is a "condiment or composition of condiments and appetizing ingredients eaten with food as a relish." Follow that? Even if you didn't, you'll relish this dish for its delightful sauce.

OYSTERS

12	oysters in shells
	rock salt
2	teaspoons vegetable oil
2	teaspoons butter
2	tablespoons thinly sliced leeks
1	cup finely shredded fresh spinach
¼	cup whipping cream
	salt and freshly ground black pepper
	dash of anisette

HOLLANDAISE SAUCE

3	egg yolks at room temperature
1	tablespoon water
2	teaspoons lemon juice
6	tablespoons butter, diced, at room temperature
	salt and white pepper
	cayenne pepper

Oysters: Shuck the oysters, reserving the deep shells and discarding the top shells and liquor. Set the shells on a bed of rock salt in a baking pan.

In a saucepan, heat the vegetable oil and butter and sauté the leeks and spinach until softened. Remove from the heat and add the whipping cream, salt and pepper, and anisette to taste. Spoon this mixture over the oysters and broil for 4 minutes. Remove from the broiler and spoon Hollandaise sauce on top. Return to the broiler and broil until hot and bubbly.

Serves 2.

Hollandaise Sauce: In the top of a double boiler over low heat, whisk egg yolks, water, and lemon juice until fluffy. Check the water in the bottom of the double boiler—it should not boil or touch the bottom of the top half of the double boiler.

Add the butter, piece by piece, making sure that each piece is incorporated before adding the next. Continue until all the butter has been used. Season with salt, white pepper, and cayenne pepper. Pour into a warm serving dish and serve at once.

Makes about 1 cup.

Captain Faunce Seafood in Montross, Virginia, is another of those spots where I stop every time I am in the neighborhood. The steamed crabs and fresh-shucked oysters are equally life-affirming.

DAMERON IMPERIAL OYSTERS

 This recipe combines oysters with two of my favorite foods: shrimp and crabmeat. The cognac sauce brings this elegant dish together nicely.

24	**oysters in shells**
¼	**cup oyster liquor**
¾	**cup heavy cream**
2	**tablespoons butter**
1½	**tablespoons all-purpose flour**
¾	**cup finely chopped cooked shrimp**
½	**cup crabmeat**
2	**tablespoons cognac**
½	**teaspoon Worcestershire sauce**
	salt and freshly ground black pepper
	Tabasco sauce
1	**cup buttered bread crumbs**
1	**tablespoon fresh minced parsley**

Scrub oyster shells under cold running water. Shuck the oysters, reserving ¼ cup of the oyster liquor and the deep shells. Dry the shells and arrange them on a baking sheet.

Warm the oyster liquor and cream in a saucepan. Melt the butter in another saucepan. Stir the flour into the butter and cook until bubbling. Remove from heat and whisk in the cream mixture. Return to heat and boil, stirring constantly, until the sauce thickens. Simmer for 3 minutes. Add the shrimp and crabmeat. Stir in the cognac and Worcestershire sauce. Add salt, pepper, and Tabasco sauce to taste. Spoon some of the sauce into each shell. Add an oyster and cover with the remaining sauce. Top with buttered bread crumbs. Bake for 5 to 10 minutes at 450°F or until the breadcrumbs are golden brown. Garnish with parsley.

Makes 24 appetizers.

Award-winning artist Mary Lou Troutman shares with us this vision of the Calvert Marine Museum in Solomons, Maryland, which includes a lovely, restored oyster buy boat, the Drum Point Lighthouse, and the surrounding salt marsh.

Painting by Mary Lou Troutman.

HOT OYSTER CANAPÉS

These oyster canapés are an adaptation of oysters on the half-shell topped with fresh sausage. I wanted an appetizer that my guests could just pop into their mouths and say, "My, my, that's good." You'll say the same.

1	**quart oysters and liquor**
1	**stick butter**
1	**loaf sliced rye bread rounds (48 rounds)**
1	**cup finely chopped fresh parsley**
1	**cup finely chopped onions**
	salt and pepper
	lemon juice
48	**rounds of sausage the diameter of a 50-cent piece, sliced ¼" thick**

Drain the oysters and discard the oyster liquor. Melt the butter in a pan. Next, brown the bread in the butter. Place the bread rounds on cookie sheets. On each bread round place a portion of parsley and onions, an oyster, a sausage round, salt, pepper, and lemon juice to taste. Broil until crisp, about 8 to 10 minutes.

Makes 48 appetizers.

I spotted this oyster Christmas tree hanging on the wall at Denton's Oyster House in Broomes Island, Maryland. Come to think of it, December is an "R" month.

CRISFIELD BILL'S OYSTERS CASINO

I tip my Crab Lab cap to my brother, Crisfield Bill, for his version of the classic clams casino recipe. Bill says, "I like the way it comes together. And it's easy, too." Thanks, Bill!

24	**oysters in shells**
3	**slices bacon, coarsely chopped**
1	**small onion, finely chopped**
1	**small green pepper, finely chopped**
1	**small rib celery, finely chopped**
1	**teaspoon lemon juice**
1	**teaspoon salt**
	freshly ground black pepper
	generous dash of Worcestershire sauce
3–4	**drops of Tabasco sauce**
½	**teaspoon seafood seasoning**
	toast points or oyster crackers

Shuck and drain the oysters, discarding oyster liquor and shells. Preheat oven to 400°F. Fry bacon in a large, heavy skillet until almost crisp. Add onion, green pepper, celery, lemon juice, salt, a generous sprinkling of black pepper, Worcestershire sauce, Tabasco sauce, and seafood seasoning. Sauté until vegetables are just tender. Arrange oysters in a single layer on a large baking sheet. Spread the bacon and vegetable mixture carefully over the tops of the oysters. Bake for 10 minutes or until the edges of the oysters begin to curl. Serve with hot toast points or a handful of oyster crackers.

Makes 24 appetizers.

This is a snapshot I took at the Chincoteague Oyster Museum on Chincoteague Island, Virginia. I think I might have courted this woman back in the mid-1980s, and you can see why.

ANGELS ON HORSEBACK

This is another of those recipes that have been around forever. I like to begin with a Beefeater Martini, followed by a couple of oysters on the half-shell and a tray of piping hot, galloping "angels." And they're off!

 1 **pint oysters and liquor**
 2 **tablespoons chopped fresh parsley**
 ½ **teaspoon salt**
    paprika
 ½ **teaspoon black pepper**
 8 **slices bacon, cut in thirds**

Drain oysters. Sprinkle with parsley, salt, paprika, and black pepper. Place an oyster on each piece of bacon. Wrap bacon around oyster and secure with a toothpick. Place oysters on a broiler pan. Broil about 4 inches from source of heat, turning several times until bacon is crisp, for 8 to 10 minutes.

Makes approximately 24 appetizers.

My buddy Bryan Hatchett took this photograph of Farr's Seafood in Messick Point, Virginia. He was on assignment covering a shipwreck in the area when he saw this oyster house and thought of me. Bryan, right back at ya.

Photograph by Bryan Hatchett

JERSEY ISLAND OYSTERS AU GRATIN

Nowadays, the term gratin is commonly applied to any dish with a topping of cheese and breadcrumbs. The term au gratin refers to any dish prepared this way.

24   **oysters in shells**
2   **tablespoons finely chopped onion**
3   **tablespoons butter, divided**
2   **tablespoons all-purpose flour**
1   **8-ounce bottle clam juice**
6   **tablespoons grated Parmigiano-Reggiano cheese, divided**
¼   **cup fine dry Italian bread crumbs**
1   **tablespoon chopped fresh cilantro dash of bottled hot pepper sauce**

Scrub oyster shells under cold running water. Shuck the oysters, discarding the oyster liquor and reserving the deep bottom shells.

In a small saucepan, cook onion in 1 tablespoon of the butter until tender. Add flour and clam juice and cook, stirring constantly, until thickened and bubbly; remove from heat. Stir in 2 tablespoons of the Parmigiano-Reggiano cheese. Melt the remaining 2 tablespoons of butter and combine with the bread crumbs, remaining 4 tablespoons of Parmigiano-Reggiano cheese, cilantro, and hot pepper sauce. Spoon 1 tablespoon of the sauce and 1 teaspoon of the crumb mixture over each oyster. Line a shallow pan with crumpled foil to keep the shells from tipping. Arrange oysters atop the foil and bake at 450°F for about 10 minutes or until heated through.

Serves 6.

Photographer Sam Gunby is one of those characters who make the Chesapeake such a nice place to live. Sam said: "I was walking on the beach at Sandy Point State Park when I saw this skipjack passing by Sandy Point Light." Always prepared, Sam set up his tripod and captured this classic image. Thanks, Sam!

Photograph by Sam Gunby.

OYSTER BRIE

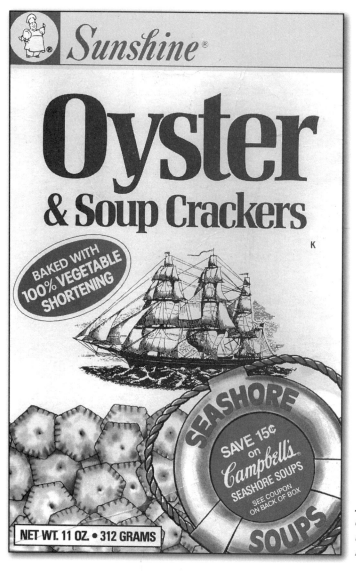

An appetizer is any small, bite-size food served before a meal to whet the appetite and stimulate the palate. This oyster brie does just that.

24   oysters in shells
3   ounces Brie cheese, sliced thin
3   tablespoons finely chopped pimento
    lemon wedges

Preheat oven to 450°F. Open oyster shells, leaving oyster in deeper half of shell. Lay a thin slice of cheese on each oyster. Sprinkle with pimento. Bake for approximately 10 minutes, or until cheese is melted and oysters are plump. Serve with lemon wedges.

Makes 24 appetizers.

Mom Schmidt raised fourteen kids on crab soup and oyster stew. I wonder how many boxes of these oyster crackers we went through. Hundreds, I'm sure—and counting.

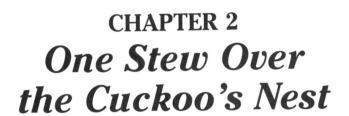

CHAPTER 2
One Stew Over the Cuckoo's Nest

Oysters
STEW
RAW
FRIED
ROASTED
AYLETT COUNTRY DAY SCHOOL
MILLERS TAVERN, VA.

Skipjack *Kathryn* Oyster Sloop Gumbo

Gumbo is a thick soup or a thin stew—depending on your point of view. Its distinguishing ingredient is okra. While the okra pods help to give gumbo its smooth, thick texture, the main flavors are provided by seafood, ham, chicken, or sometimes all of the above.

1   3-pound chicken, cut into serving
      pieces
      salt and pepper
2   tablespoons vegetable oil
2   tablespoons all-purpose flour

1   onion, finely chopped
1   tomato, finely sliced
2   quarts hot water
¼   teaspoon cayenne pepper
1   pint oysters
1   package (10 ounces) frozen okra
      fresh parsley
2   tablespoons filé powder
      steamed rice

Season chicken pieces with salt and pepper. Heat oil in frying pan. Brown chicken in oil and remove to a serving plate. Add flour to remaining liquid in pan and brown very slowly, stirring constantly, until the roux is a rich brown. Add onion and cook until tender. Add tomato. Return chicken to pan, add hot water and cayenne pepper, and simmer until chicken is tender, about 30 minutes. Remove chicken, debone and return meat to pan. Add oysters, okra, and parsley and simmer for 20 minutes more. Remove from heat and add filé powder. Serve in large soup bowls over steamed rice.
   Serves 6.

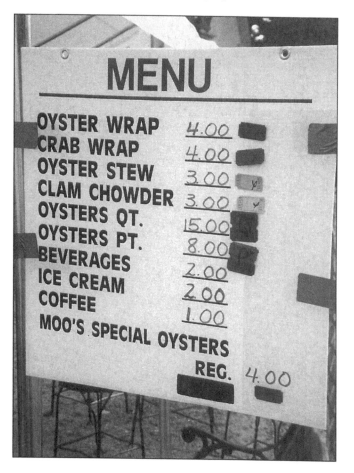

MENU

OYSTER WRAP   4.00
CRAB WRAP   4.00
OYSTER STEW   3.00
CLAM CHOWDER   3.00
OYSTERS QT.   15.00
OYSTERS PT.   8.00
BEVERAGES   2.00
ICE CREAM   2.00
COFFEE   1.00
MOO'S SPECIAL OYSTERS
               REG. 4.00

I spotted this sign while visiting the Urbanna Oyster Festival 2001. The first thing I look for at oyster festivals is oyster stew. Then I order a bowl and, well, I become happy.

OLD OYSTER LANE CORN CHOWDER

Flecked with green chilies and laced with golden corn, this soup makes a fine supper with a salad, some cheese, apples, bread and, of course, a glass of chilled chardonnay.

1	**quart milk**
1	**package (3 ounces) cream cheese, cubed**
1	**can (16 ounces) cream-style corn**
6	**strips bacon, diced**
1	**large onion, chopped**
4	**medium potatoes, cooked, peeled, diced**
1	**can (4 ounces) chopped green chilies, drained, divided**
½	**teaspoon salt**
½	**teaspoon cayenne pepper**
1	**quart select oysters**
½	**cup sour cream**

Place milk in large saucepan and slowly bring to a boil. Lower heat; add cream cheese cubes and corn. Cook, stirring often, over low heat, until cream cheese has melted. Set aside.

In small skillet, cook bacon and onion until bacon is crisp. Drain off excess bacon fat and discard. Add bacon, onion and potatoes to milk mixture. Reserve 3 teaspoons green chilies for garnish and add remaining green chilies to milk mixture along with salt and cayenne pepper. Heat through. Adjust seasonings. Add oysters to hot soup and cook just until edges of oysters curl. Ladle soup into bowls. Top each serving with a dollop of sour cream; scatter reserved chilies over sour cream.

Serves 8.

While driving my old Pontiac around Virginia's lower Eastern Shore I discovered Oyster, an authentic fishing village clustered around a small harbor, complete with watermen in white rubber boots, flocks of seagulls, and this sign. Guess what I had for lunch!

OYSTERS AND BRIE SOUP

Brie is probably the most famous French cheese. It has a long history and was made as early as the 13th century. Brie is named after the district of La Brie, along the Marne Valley near Paris. This cheese is smooth and satiny and—when combined with oysters, white wine and cream—it's heavenly.

1	**stick butter**
¼	**cup all-purpose flour**
8	**ounces brie, rind removed**
2	**cups milk**
1	**cup heavy cream**
1	**cup good white wine**
2	**teaspoons Tabasco sauce**
¼	**teaspoon salt**
½	**teaspoon coarsely ground black pepper**
1	**pint oysters and liquor**
2	**tablespoons finely chopped green onions**
¼	**teaspoon dried thyme**

In a medium saucepan melt butter over medium heat. Whisk in flour. Add brie, milk, cream, and wine. Stir constantly until cheese is melted. Season with Tabasco, salt, and pepper. Bring to a boil and add oysters and liquor, green onion, and thyme. Cook until oysters curl, about 5 minutes.

Serves 4.

I'm kind of an aficionado of signage, especially when they advertise four of my favorite foods. This day, I did a cartwheel.

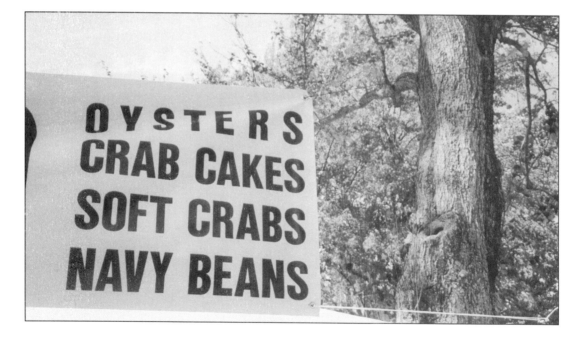

OLD HAMPTON OYSTER STEW

This recipe was created for a Sunday brunch. I wanted to serve a dish that no one else did, and this one is unique. My guests always ask for the recipe and say they never tasted anything like it. I got the idea from Chef Ben at Harpoon Larry's.

1½ **pounds potatoes, peeled and diced**
 4 **ounces andouille sausage, sliced**
 3 **tablespoons butter, divided**
½ **cup heavy cream, divided**
 1 **pint oysters**
 1 **tablespoon olive oil**
½ **cup chopped onions**
  salt and freshly ground black pepper
 1 **clove garlic, chopped**
 2 **tablespoons finely chopped parsley leaves**
  Worcestershire sauce
  Tabasco sauce
  juice of one lemon

Place the pototatoes in a saucepan and cover with water. Season with salt and bring to a boil. Reduce to simmer and cook until the potatoes are fork tender. Drain.

In a small sauté pan over medium heat, fry the sausage until crispy, about 5 minutes.

Place the potatoes back in the saucepan and add 1 tablespoon of the butter and ¼ cup of the cream. Mash the potatoes until smooth and season with salt and pepper. Set aside and keep warm.

Drain the oysters, reserving the liquor. Set the oysters aside. Add the oil to a large sauté pan over medium heat. When the oil is hot, add the onions. Season with salt and pepper and sauté for 2 to 3 minutes. Add the garlic and parsley and cook for 2 more minutes, and then add the reserved oyster liquor, Worcestershire sauce, and lemon juice. Bring the liquid to a boil and reduce to a simmer. Cook for 4 to 5 minutes, until the liquid thickens.

Stir the remaining butter and cream into the potatoes in the saucepan.

Season the oysters with salt and pepper and add them to the oyster liquor mixture in the sauté pan. Simmer for 2 minutes or until the oysters' edges curl.

To serve, mound the potatoes in the center of each bowl. Spoon the oyster mixture around the potatoes and top with the sausage slices.

Serves 6.

Photograph by Vince Lupo.

*C*hef Ben Koffler at Harpoon Larry's in Hampton Virginia, presents a bowl of oyster stew for my enjoyment, and enjoy it I did.

OLD VIRGINIE OYSTER STEW

This recipe comes from years of following Pop Schmidt around the kitchen at Christmas time and watching carefully, noting everything that went into the pot. I now realize that the dried thyme is what brings this stew together. See if you don't agree.

1	quart oysters
1	cup oyster liquor
1	cup water
½	cup (1 stick) butter, divided
½	cup chopped celery
⅓	cup chopped green onions
1	small onion, chopped
2	cloves garlic, chopped
1	teaspoon dried thyme
½	teaspoon salt
¼	teaspoon pepper
4	cups milk

Simmer the oysters in the oyster liquor and water until the edges curl. Remove from heat and drain, reserving the liquor. In ¼ cup of the butter, sauté the celery, green onions, onions, garlic, thyme, salt and pepper for about 5 minutes. Then stir in the milk. Add the oysters to the sauce along with ½ cup of the reserved oyster liquor. Bring the stew to a boil and serve. Dot the serving bowls with chunks of the remaining butter as you pour.

Serves 8.

I spotted this sign in Willis Wharf, Virginia. The building sits at the water's edge in an area that turns to the sea for its livelihood. I inquired about oysters and was quickly accommodated.

SEASIDE OYSTER STEW

I love oyster stew, and this recipe makes a really hearty one. The liquor from freshly shucked oysters is the key to a good oyster stew. I admit to preferring the Seaside oysters from Virginia's lower Eastern Shore, but I'm not too picky.

4   tablespoons butter
¼   teaspoon anchovy paste
1   tablespoon Dijon mustard
3   cups finely chopped celery
1   quart heavy cream
1   quart oysters and liquor
¼   cup dry sherry
    salt and freshly ground pepper
    paprika
    chopped parsley

Melt the butter in a large saucepan and whisk in anchovy paste and mustard. Add the celery and cook until tender. Stir in the cream and bring to a boil. Add the oysters, liquor, and sherry and heat until the edges of the oysters begin to curl. Season with salt and pepper to taste. Serve in warmed bowls and garnish with paprika and parsley.

Serves 6.

The Chesapeake side of the Eastern Shore is known as "Bayside" in the local parlance. The Atlantic side is called Seaside. (A series of barrier islands protects the Seaside from the ocean's waves.) When I can find oysters from the Seaside, that's what I buy.

JACKSON CREEK OYSTER SOUP

Oysters might just be everybody's favorite shellfish. They come in all kinds of shapes and sizes. The flavors vary as much as the sizes, depending upon where the oysters are harvested. And when you flavor up any oysters with clam juice and sherry, why, it's magic!

4	tablespoons clarified butter
½	cup finely diced celery
½	cup finely chopped onion
½	teaspoon Worcestershire sauce
½	teaspoon Tabasco sauce
¼	teaspoon celery salt
1	pint oysters and liquor
3½	cups clam juice
½	cup medium-dry sherry
2	cups half-and-half
	freshly ground black pepper

In a large, heavy saucepan, heat the butter over moderate heat, add the celery and onion, and cook until softened but not browned, 3 to 5 minutes. Add the Worcestershire and Tabasco sauces, celery salt, oysters and liquor, clam juice, sherry, and half-and-half. Cook, stirring occasionally, until hot (do not boil), 4 to 5 minutes. Season with pepper to taste and serve at once.

Serves 4.

A sign of our times is the "God Bless America" that appears on many billboards, cars, and buildings all around Bay country. Another sign that brings tears to my eyes is the one for Salty Oysters.

CHURCH SUPPER OYSTER STEW

Church suppers around the Bay are common, and the number of oysters consumed at church affairs . . . well, no wonder we have a shortage! I keep this recipe close by—you never know when you'll get married again.

3   **gallons oysters and liquor**
2   **pounds butter**
4   **gallons hot milk**
5   **tablespoons salt**
2   **teaspoons pepper**
1   **teaspoon seafood seasoning**
1   **tablespoon paprika**

Heat the oysters and liquor for about 5 minutes, or until the edges of the oysters begin to curl. Add butter, hot milk, salt, pepper, seafood seasoning, and paprika. Serve immediately.
Serves 100 (1-cup servings).

There are as many oyster festivals around the Bay as there are crab cook-offs. When I see a sign like this, I say, "Bring it on!"

Photograph by Vince Lupo

41

OYSTER AND CELERY SOUP

I stopped debating the origin of this sump-tuous soup years ago. Who cares where it came from? It tastes great! I was raised on it and continue to prepare it regularly. This is also an easy dish to prepare, and it can be pointed up with imaginative seasonings, vegetables, or even other shellfish. Have fun. Be creative.

1 **cup diced celery**
1 **tablespoon chopped onion**
2 **cups water**
2 **tablespoons chopped pimientos**
 dash cayenne pepper
 dash Tabasco sauce
1 **tablespoon butter**
1 **tablespoon all-purpose flour**
1 **pint half-and-half**
1 **pint oysters**

2 **egg yolks, beaten**
1 **teaspoon lemon juice**
 toast points

In a saucepan, cook celery and onion in water until tender. Stir in pimientos, cayenne pepper and Tabasco sauce and remove from heat. In a large skillet, melt butter, add flour, and stir until smooth. Add half-and-half and stir constantly until the mixture boils. Add oysters and celery mixture and heat until the edges of the oysters begin to curl. Whisk in egg yolks slowly, stirring constantly. Add lemon juice and stir until incorporated. Serve at once over toast points.

Serves 4.

GROWN ON PRIVATE BEDS OF COX BROS., 1935-36 IN WICOMICO RIVER, NANTICOKE, MD.

Oysters eat day and night, and the gills siphon an average of 20 to 50 gallons of water per day. Oysters in the Chesapeake reach marketable size in about three years. Look at these beauties grown in private beds. I'll take a dozen.

OYSTER STEW WITH ARTICHOKE HEARTS

The artichoke was discovered centuries ago by the Arabs, but it was first cultivated in 15th-century Italy. Connoisseurs recognize that the smaller the artichoke, the better the flavor. They also know how well artichokes and oysters go together.

2	tablespoons butter
2	tablespoons all-purpose flour
2	cups milk
1	cup heavy cream
1	cup quartered artichoke hearts
½	cup clam juice
1	pint oysters and liquor
1	teaspoon salt
½	teaspoon white pepper
1	teaspoon dried parsley
	pinch of tarragon
2	teaspoons Tabasco sauce

In a medium stockpot, melt butter. Whisk in flour. Over medium heat, add milk and whisk until mixture is thick. Add cream, artichoke hearts, clam juice, oysters and liquor, salt, pepper, parsley, and tarragon. Heat until the broth thickens and oysters curl, about 8 minutes. Add Tabasco sauce just before serving.

Serves 4.

*D*ecisions, decisions . . . I don't know what to do. Wait, I know: Give me some of each!

43

DAYS OF POWER OYSTER CHOWDER

 *Chowder wouldn't be chowder without biscuits to sop up every last tantalizing mouthful.*

- ½ cup chopped onion
- ½ cup sliced celery
- ¼ cup butter
- 1 pint oysters, drained and liquor reserved
- 3 cups oyster liquor and milk (add enough milk to the oyster liquor to make 3 cups)
- 1 cup cooked, diced potatoes
- 1 can (8 ounces) whole kernel corn, undrained
- 1½ teaspoons salt
- ¼ teaspoon pepper
- 1 cup half-and-half
- 1 tablespoon chopped fresh parsley
- ½ teaspoon paprika

In a saucepan, sauté onion and celery in butter until tender. Add oyster liquor/milk mixture, potatoes, corn, salt, pepper, and half-and-half. Heat, stirring occasionally. Add oysters and heat for 3 to 5 minutes longer, or until edges of oysters curl. Do not allow to boil. Garnish with chopped parsley and paprika.

Serves 6.

An old Schmidt family saying: Oysters speak louder when cooked in a chowder.

OYSTER SOUP CHALLENGE

Help Choose The

Best Oyster Soup In Maryland

11:00 am - 2:00 pm

Tickets: $8.00 per person

DON'T MISS IT!

SETTER'S POINT GOLDEN OYSTER STEW

When friends Barb and Dan Kuebler served this golden stew one evening as an appetizer (preceding a huge, whole rockfish roasted on a plank), it was made with rich, heavy cream. I like to cut the cream with whole milk, but you can choose for yourself. Thanks, Barb and Dan!

½ cup chopped onion
½ cup sliced celery
2 tablespoons butter
2 cups sliced fresh mushrooms
2 tablespoons all-purpose flour
2 cups milk
1 cup (4 ounces) shredded sharp cheddar cheese
1 can (10.5 ounces) cream of potato soup, undiluted
1 jar (2 ounces) diced pimiento, undrained
¼ teaspoon salt
¼ teaspoon pepper
¼ teaspoon Tabasco sauce
1 pint oysters and liquor
   pinch saffron

In a saucepan, sauté onion and celery in butter until tender. Add mushrooms and cook for 2 minutes. Add flour and cook for 1 minute, stirring constantly. Gradually add milk; cook over medium heat, stirring until mixture is thickened and bubbly. Stir in cheese, potato soup, pimiento, salt, pepper, and Tabasco sauce; cook over medium heat, stirring often, until cheese melts and mixture is thoroughly heated. Add oysters and liquor; reduce heat and simmer until edges of oysters curl. Add saffron, stir until combined, and serve at once.

Serves 6.

Throughout Chesapeake country, roadside markets must advertise to stay alive. This "Come into my kitchen, I want you to meet my oysters" kind of sign extracted $38 from my wallet.

EDYTHE'S CLAM AND OYSTER BISQUE

Photograph by Vince Lupo.

There's something almost playful about the combination of ingredients in this bisque. The result is a fortifying luncheon treat or a whimsical transition to an entrée of, say, pork tenderloin surrounded by boiled new potatoes and glazed carrots.

1	**pint clams**
1	**pint oysters and liquor**
1	**stick butter**
2	**strips bacon, chopped**
1	**teaspoon chopped fresh parsley**
½	**cup chopped onion**
⅓	**cup chopped green pepper**
1	**medium potato, peeled and diced**
¼	**cup chopped celery**
2	**small carrots, peeled and chopped**
1	**teaspoon salt**
¼	**teaspoon pepper**
	thyme to taste
1	**teaspoon Tabasco sauce**
½	**teaspoon Worcestershire sauce**
3	**cups half-and-half, scalded**
3	**cups hot water**

Combine clams, oysters and liquor, butter, bacon, parsley, onion, green pepper, potato, celery, and carrots in a large saucepan. Simmer about 1 hour. Pour mixture into container of electric blender and process until smooth. Return to the saucepan and stir in salt, pepper, thyme, Tabasco sauce, Worcestershire sauce, half-and-half, and water. Heat thoroughly and serve immediately.

Serves 10.

I can sit and watch oysters being shucked all day, especially when the person doing the shucking is my friend and I'm allowed to slurp away at will.

46

POTOMAC RUN OYSTER AND SPINACH SOUP

Cooks love to be imaginative and will seize every opportunity to experiment with different flavors and textures. Wait till you taste what spinach does to oyster soup. My, my!

½   cup finely chopped onion
2   cloves garlic, minced
½   cup butter
1   pint oysters, chopped
½   cup all-purpose flour
1½   quarts half-and-half
2   cups chicken broth
2   packages (10 ounces each) frozen
       spinach, thawed and puréed
1   teaspoon salt
     pepper to taste

In a large saucepan, sauté onion and garlic in butter until tender; add oysters and cook until edges begin to curl. Blend in flour and cook until bubbly. Gradually add half-and-half and cook, stirring constantly, until thickened. Stir in chicken broth and spinach; bring to a boil. Remove from heat and season with salt and pepper.
     Serves 8.

Fresh oysters may be purchased in three forms: live in the shell, shucked fresh, and canned. While canned oysters taste good, they can't compare in flavor to the freshly shucked oyster— and that all-important oyster liquor.

Photograph by Vince Lupo

47

MAIN GATE CRAB & OYSTER BISQUE

This recipe has been in the family for nearly a century and was one my mother served as the first course of our elaborate Christmas dinners. I find it perfect as part of a casual lunch including fruit salad and hush puppies.

1   quart oysters and liquor
1   tablespoon butter
1   cup chopped onion
½   cup chopped celery
½   cup chopped green pepper
2   cloves garlic, minced
½   cup all-purpose flour
1¾ cups chicken broth
½   teaspoon dried thyme
1   bay leaf
½   cup sliced green onions
1   pint half-and-half
1   pound lump crabmeat
¼   teaspoon salt
    freshly ground black pepper

Drain the oysters in a colander over a bowl, reserving 1 cup oyster liquor. In a large Dutch oven, sauté onion, celery, green pepper, and garlic over medium heat for 5 minutes. Add flour and cook for 1 minute, stirring constantly. Gradually add reserved oyster liquor and chicken broth and whisk until blended. Stir in thyme and bay leaf and bring to a boil. Add oysters, green onions, and half-and-half; cook until edges of oysters curl. Gently stir in crabmeat and salt and cook until thoroughly heated. Discard bay leaf. Sprinkle with black pepper.

Serves 6.

As I travel around the Chesapeake Bay, visiting the numerous festivals and fairs celebrating the oyster, I always look for signs like this, which usually lead to me purchasing both pints and quarts.

COLES POINT OYSTER STEW

"Beautiful soup! Who cares for fish, game, or any other dish? Who would not give all else for two pennyworth only of beautiful soup?"
—LEWIS CARROLL, *ALICE IN WONDERLAND*

1   **pint oysters and liquor**
4   **tablespoons butter**
1   **teaspoon Worcestershire sauce**
1   **teaspoon celery salt**
1   **quart milk**
    salt and pepper
    paprika

Drain oysters, reserving liquor. Place butter, Worcestershire sauce, and celery salt in a 2-quart saucepan. Cook slowly for 1 or 2 minutes. Add oysters and liquor, and simmer until oyster edges start to curl. Add milk, salt, and pepper to taste. Heat thoroughly, but do not boil. Pour into bowls and garnish with paprika.

Serves 4.

While eating my way around the Chesapeake back in the early eighties, I photographed Sonny Allen's Oyster House. I returned in 2003 and took a number of new photos. These piles of oyster shells are now higher than the trucks!

CHOPTANK OYSTER STEW

Recipes for oyster stew are traditionally simple. Ingredients other than oysters tend to be so minimal that the oysters are essentially the soup. Use freshly shucked oysters for the ultimate in flavor. Don't forget it!

4 tablespoons butter
½ teaspoon Worcestershire sauce
   dash of celery salt
½ cup diced celery
1 pint oysters and liquor
2 cups hot milk
¼ teaspoon salt
   dash of pepper
2 tablespoons sherry

Melt butter in a small saucepan over low heat; stir in Worcestershire sauce, celery salt, celery, and oysters and liquor. Heat slowly until edges of oysters begin to curl. Add hot milk and season with salt and pepper. Stir in sherry; heat thoroughly but do not boil. Serve immediately.

Serves 4.

If you want to try some great-tasting oyster stew, pay a visit to the Urbanna (Virginia) Oyster Festival and sample a bowl of the Ware Academy's. It's mighty good.

CREAM OF OYSTER-SPINACH SOUP

When I ran into Betty Mitchell at the Chesapeake Bay Maritime Museum in St. Michaels, Maryland, she told me about this recipe. I couldn't wait to get home and give it a try. I love this dish because it can be prepared in a jiffy, and because it tastes like a million bucks. Why, it's rich as a Rockefeller! Thanks, Betty.

½	cup butter
2	ribs celery, chopped
1	medium onion, chopped
3	packages (10 ounces each) frozen chopped spinach, thawed
1	cup milk
1½	quarts oysters and liquor
2	tablespoons steak sauce
1	teaspoon salt
½	teaspoon garlic salt
	dash of pepper
2	cups heavy cream

In a Dutch oven, melt butter. Sauté celery and onion in butter until translucent. Press all liquid from spinach and add it with the milk. Add oysters and liquor and cook over low heat until edges of oysters curl. Add steak sauce, salt, garlic salt, and pepper. Cook until the mixture begins to boil; remove from heat. Purée in a blender and return to pot. Add heavy cream and again bring almost to a boil. Serve immediately.

Serves 8 to 10.

*W*hy buy a T-shirt when you could buy three bowls of this wonderful stew?

WEDGED IN THE ICE OYSTER STEW

This is exactly the kind of hearty soup that every waterman dreams of after an invigorating winter's day of cutting through skim-ice. Serve it with dark Guinness draft and a crusty loaf of fresh-baked bread.

    1   quart oysters and liquor
    1   pound country sausage
    2   green onions, chopped
        salt and pepper
        dash of garlic powder

Drain oysters; reserve liquor. Form thin sausage patties and fry until well done; crumble them into bite-size pieces and reserve the fat. In an iron skillet, place 3 tablespoons sausage fat, sausage pieces, oysters, and the reserved oyster liquor with enough water added to it to make 1 quart. Cook until oyster edges begin to curl. Add green onions. Season with salt, pepper, and a dash of garlic powder.

Serves 6 to 8.

Bay Weekly, my favorite Chesapeake country newspaper, holds a yearly readers' poll. Apparently, your choice for the Bay's best oysters is McGarvey's saloon, located at the City Dock in downtown Annapolis. I might just agree with you.

SHRIMP AND OYSTER JAM-BUH-LI-YAH

Jambalaya is one of those dishes that changes every time you make it. The last time I made this version, I used a full pound of sausage, and I didn't hear one complaint.

2   cups raw rice
2   bay leaves
½   pint oysters, drained and liquor
    reserved
½   pound sausage meat
¼   cup vegetable oil
¼   cup all-purpose flour
1   large onion, sliced
¼   cup minced green pepper
½   cup minced celery
½   cup stewed tomatoes
1   clove garlic, minced
    1 tablespoon butter
1   pound shrimp, cooked and shelled
1   teaspoon Worcestershire sauce
    salt and pepper
1   tablespoon minced fresh parsley

In a large saucepan, place rice, bay leaves, and oyster liquor with enough water to make 1 quart of liquid. Bring to a boil and then lower heat and simmer until rice is done, about 20 minutes.

While rice is cooking, sauté the sausage in a large skillet. Remove from pan and drain on paper towels. Discard all but 1 tablespoon of the fat. Add vegetable oil to the pan and stir in flour. Over medium heat, stir until mixture is golden brown. Add onion, green pepper, and celery and sauté until soft. Add tomatoes and cook for 5 minutes. In a small pan, sauté garlic in butter until tender. When rice is done, remove bay leaves and add onion and garlic mixtures, oysters, shrimp, Worcestershire sauce, and salt and pepper to taste.

Place in a tureen and garnish with parsley. Serves 4 to 6.

Whenever I see signs like this during my travels around Chesapeake country, my credit cards shake in their proverbial little credit-card-size boots: Visa, MasterCard or what have you. I must agree with Captain John Smith, who wrote that in Virginia, "We were never more merry nor fed on more plenty of good oysters."

OYSTER AND GUINNESS SOUP

Lotteries are as old as clocks. The ancient mariners started the tradition of lotteries by betting on the exact time the anchor would be secured upon arrival at a new port, which would be determined afterwards by the official notation in the captain's log. I'm going to guess when this soup will next come off the heat and time my arrival appropriately!

1	**stick butter, divided**
2	**shallots, chopped**
²⁄₃	**cup dry white wine**
½	**cup all-purpose flour**
1¼	**cups fish stock (or store-bought clam juice)**
1	**pint oysters and liquor**
1¼	**cups Guinness Extra Stout**
²⁄₃	**cup heavy cream**
	salt and pepper
1	**tablespoon chopped fresh parsley**

In a saucepan, melt half the butter. Add the shallots and cook over medium heat until soft. Add the wine and simmer for 3 minutes.

Meanwhile, in another saucepan, make a roux by melting the remaining butter, whisking in the flour, and cooking for 1 minute over medium heat. Gradually mix the fish stock into the roux and stir constantly until the sauce is creamy. Add the sauce to the shallots and season with salt and pepper.

Drain the oysters and add their liquor and the Guinness to the soup, and bring the soup to a boil. Reduce the heat and stir in the cream and the oysters. Continue to cook over low heat until the oysters curl. Garnish with chopped parsley.

Serves 4.

*A*nti-gambling laws made "the numbers" illegal, but as time passed, and the need for additional public revenues increased, the laws were relaxed to allow states to hold their own lotteries. I wouldn't dream of playing a number without my Lucky Oyster Book.

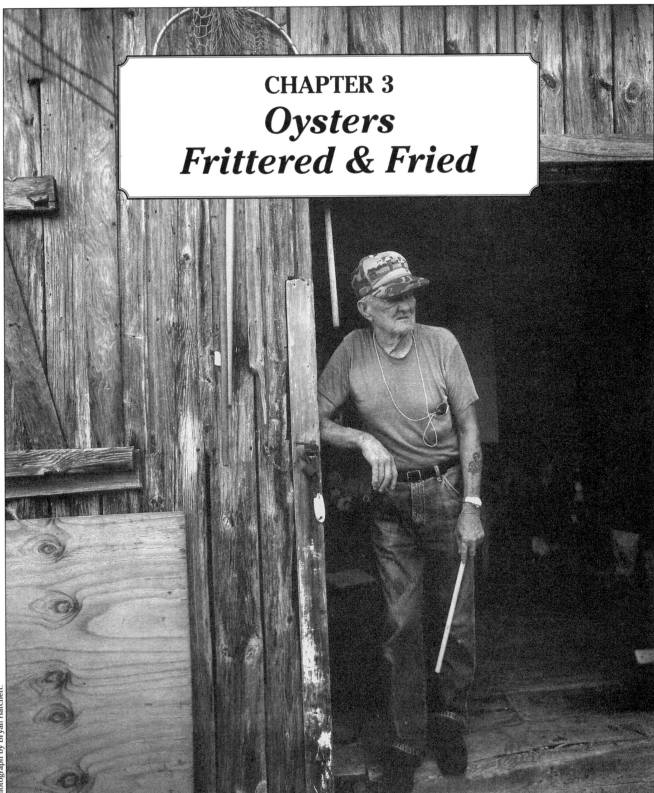

CHAPTER 3
Oysters Frittered & Fried

DEEP-FRIED OYSTERS WITH FLUFFY HORSERADISH SAUCE

In today's home kitchen, chefs can fry oysters to perfection in professional-quality fryers. Digital technology allows for precise temperature control, and the basins and baskets are usually stainless steel for easy cleaning. Me, I use the simple Fry-Daddy—just fill it to the mark with peanut oil and plug it in.

- 1   **cup yellow cornmeal**
       salt and pepper
- 1   **pint oysters**
- 4   **cups peanut oil for frying**

FLUFFY HORSERADISH SAUCE
- ¼   **cup prepared horseradish**
- 1   **tablespoon vinegar**
- 1   **teaspoon sugar**
- ½   **cup heavy cream, whipped**

Season cornmeal with salt and pepper to taste. Drain the oysters and dredge them in the cornmeal mixture. Heat the oil in a skillet or deep fat fryer to 350°F. Add the oysters and cook until nicely browned, about 1 minute.

Fluffy Horseradish Sauce: Combine all ingredients and mix well.

Serves 4.

Oysters, like clams, vary from one coast to another. East Coast oysters—namely, the American or Eastern oysters that are variously called Choptanks, Chincoteagues, Lynnhavens or Bay oysters—are so scarce that this gastronomical treat carries an astronomical price tag.

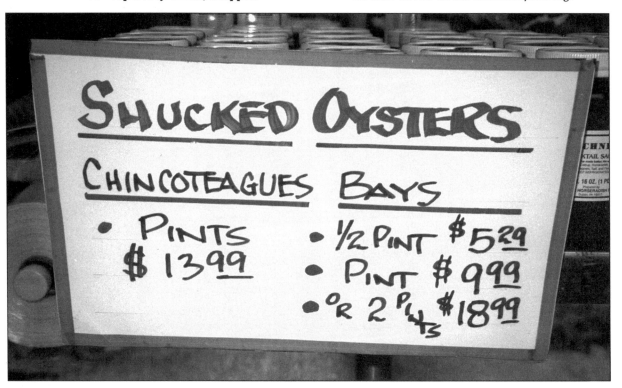

NANTICOKE OYSTER FRITTERS

Fritters are anchored by bits of food—usually corn, crab or oysters—suspended in batter and deep-fried. The name reflects the method of cooking, as you can indeed fritter away time dropping spoonfuls of fritter batter into the pot. It's interesting to note that apple fritters have appeared in cookbooks since the 1300s.

1	pint oysters and liquor
2	cups all-purpose flour
1	tablespoon baking powder
1½	teaspoons salt
½	teaspoon seafood seasoning
2	eggs, beaten
1	cup milk
1	tablespoon butter, melted
	peanut oil for frying
	lemon slices

Drain oysters and set aside. Discard the liquor. In a large bowl, combine the flour, baking powder, salt, and seafood seasoning. In a small bowl, combine the beaten eggs, milk, and melted butter. Fold the wet ingredients into the dry and stir until smooth. Add the oysters. Drop the batter by teaspoonfuls into oil heated to 350°F and fry for about 3 minutes or until golden brown. Drain on absorbent paper. Garnish with lemon slices.

Serves 6.

People eating large quantities of oyster fritters have been known to have their tongues curl. They have also been accused of dressing oddly and barking at the moon. Ruff-ruff!

EASTERN SHORE OYSTER FRITTERS

Maritime Artifacts, Oyster Farming & Seafood Industry

See exhibits featuring historic relics depicting the work of the waterman and life in the fishing village of Chincoteague. Examine the oystering tools, mostly handmade, and the largest oyster ever recorded around Chincoteague. Visit the sight and sound diorama that explains oystering - from breeding, growing, harvesting, packing, and shipping.

These fritters are dramatic-looking, delicious, fun to eat, and so much fun to make that you'll make them often.

1   **pint oysters and liquor**
½   **cup evaporated milk**
1   **cup pancake mix**
2   **tablespoons cornmeal**
1   **teaspoon salt**
    black pepper
    cooking oil

Drain oysters, reserving liquor. In a bowl, combine oysters, milk, pancake mix, cornmeal, salt and pepper. Mix well. (Batter will be thick. If it becomes too thick on standing, thin with oyster liquor.) Heat oil in a large frying pan. Drop batter into hot oil by tablespoonsful, making sure to include two oysters in each portion. Cook until golden brown on one side, 1 to 2 minutes. Turn carefully and brown the other side.

Makes about 12.

The Oyster & Maritime Museum located on Virginia's lower Eastern Shore is a great place to explore the past and understand the present. This oyster-fishing heritage is fascinating for all those who hanker for knowledge of the Chesapeake's history, and the museum itself is a magical place—a sort of time machine for the imagination.

HIGHWAY CHURCH FRIED OYSTERS

The last time I started planning for a small party, the guest list (memorized, of course) leaped from 12 to 32 real fast. No problem! I cut this recipe in half, rounded out the meal with calico slaw and a country-kitchen dessert—you get the idea. It was a traditional Shore supper, and we savored it with emotion.

4	tablespoons salt
1	tablespoon pepper
2	dozen eggs, beaten
1	pint milk
3	gallons oysters
1	gallon dry bread crumbs
	oil for frying

Mix salt, pepper, eggs, and milk in a large bowl. Dip oysters in this mixture and then roll them in bread crumbs. Heat oil to 375° and fry oysters for about 2 minutes, until golden brown. Drain on absorbent paper and serve immediately with ketchup or another sauce.

Serves approximately 100 (6 to 8 oysters each).

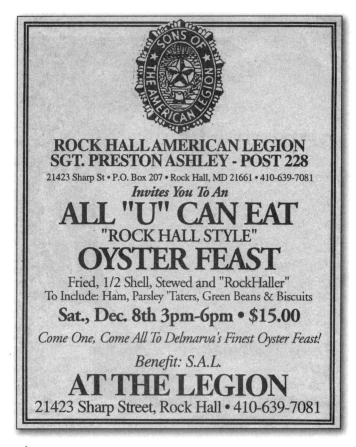

An invitation to an all-you-can-eat oyster feast is just the ticket when you're in Bay country and you're hungry. I'm hungry already, and all I did was read this simple advert from the American Legion. Will I see you there? (Hint: I'll be standing very close to the shucking table.)

LORE HOUSE OYSTER FRITTERS

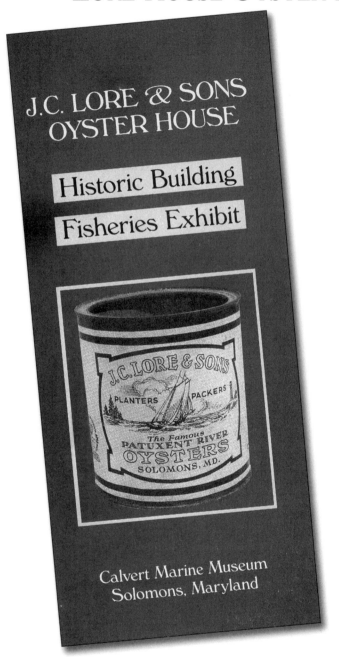

J.C. LORE & SONS
OYSTER HOUSE

Historic Building

Fisheries Exhibit

J.C. LORE & SONS
PLANTERS   PACKERS
The Famous
PATUXENT RIVER
OYSTERS
SOLOMONS, MD.

Calvert Marine Museum
Solomons, Maryland

To say that oyster fritters should be served only as a side dish is a Sunday sin. One of my favorite meals is a breakfast of fritters. I melt a dab of butter on them, sprinkle them with salt and pepper, and then add a drizzle of Karo syrup, proving that this classic fritter recipe need not be limited to side-dish status.

1	**cup pancake mix**
1	**teaspoon baking powder**
1	**pint oysters and liquor**
1	**egg**
2	**tablespoons finely chopped onion**
	salt and pepper
¼	**cup vegetable oil**

Combine pancake mix, baking powder, oysters and liquor, egg, and onion; mix well. Add salt and pepper to taste. Heat oil in a frying pan, and drop mixture by tablespoonfuls into the hot (but not smoking) oil. Fry until golden brown on one side; turn and fry on other side until done. Drain well on absorbent paper and serve hot.

Makes about 20 fritters.

This oyster house dates from 1934. It is built on a huge pile of oyster shells that were discarded over the years at Solomons, Maryland. In 1980, the Calvert Marine Museum purchased the building and the packing equipment inside. The packing room and a shucking room have been restored to their original appearance. Much of the equipment used by J. C. Lore & Sons remains exactly where it was when the building functioned as a working oyster-packing house.

DAMIEN HEANEY'S IRISH OYSTERS

Executive Chef Damien Heaney of Legends Restaurant on Maryland's Eastern Shore suggests that you use plenty of butter for this dish—that way you won't have to turn them while they're frying. I like the way he thinks.

1 **quart oysters and liquor**
4 **eggs, beaten**
1 **cup all-purpose flour**
  clarified butter
  salt and pepper
  lemon wedges
  sprigs of parsley

Drain oysters, reserving liquor. Combine eggs, flour, salt, pepper, and enough oyster liquor to make a smooth batter (add water if necessary). Heat the butter in a frying pan. Dip the oysters in the batter and fry until golden brown. Serve with lemon wedges and garnish with parsley.
Serves 6.

Skipping oyster shells, like cooking, is an art. I remember as a kid tossing a shell across the water on the Western Shore. Years later, I was on Tilghman Island and caught that same shell as it bounced across the Bay—yeah, I got an arm on me.

GENERAL TANUKI'S CURRY FRIED OYSTERS

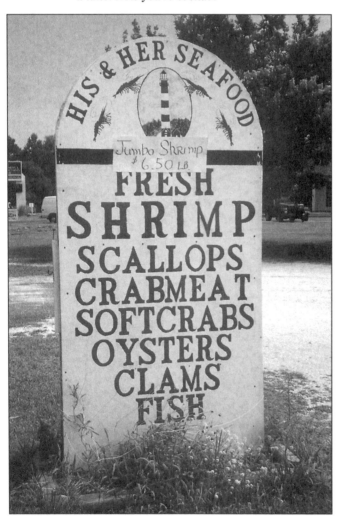 *To single fry oysters, it's important that only one oyster is breaded at a time (some unscrupulous restaurants have battered two or three together—gasp!). More than one oyster will mean that the oysters will get soggy, and you don't want that. Similarly, when frying the oysters, don't crowd the pan; do only a few at a time. Now you're cookin'!*

DIPPING SAUCE

- 1 **tablespoon olive oil**
- **S & B Mild Golden Curry sauce mix (Note: You can find S & B at gourmet markets and specialty stores.)**
- 1 **can (8 ounces) coconut milk**
- 8 **ounces heavy cream**
- ½ **cup white wine**

OYSTERS

- 24 **oysters and liquor**
- 2 **cups yellow cornmeal**
- 1½ **cups all-purpose flour**
- 3 **tablespoons curry powder**
- **pinch of salt**
- **hot oil for deep frying**

Dipping sauce: In a saucepan, heat the olive oil and sauté the curry paste until it starts to stick to the pan. Add the white wine and stir. Remove from the heat and whisk in the coconut milk and heavy cream. Return to low heat until heated through. Pour this cream sauce through a sieve (parts of it will be too chunky) and keep warm.

Oysters: In a medium-size bowl, combine cornmeal, curry powder, and salt. Shuck the oysters and discard the liquor and shells. Dip each oyster in the cornmeal mixture and deep-fry just until lightly browned. Place the dipping sauce in individual dishes and serve immediately!
Serves 6.

*J*ust a glance at this sign reminded me: I have a lot of reasons to stop at His & Her Seafood.

CHESAPEAKE APPRECIATION DAYS PAN-FRIED OYSTERS

 Anyone who appreciates Chesapeake cooking will like the addition of Bay spice to this dish. It points up the taste nicely without overpowering the oyster flavor. My preferred brands are Old Bay and J.O.—sprinkle some on the oysters as soon as you remove them from the pan.

1	pint oysters and liquor
2	eggs, beaten
2	tablespoons milk
½	teaspoon seafood seasoning
1	teaspoon salt
	dash pepper
1½	cups dry bread crumbs
1½	cups all-purpose flour
	peanut oil for frying
	lemon wedges

TARTAR SAUCE

1	tablespoon capers, drained
1	tablespoon finely chopped dill pickles
1	tablespoon finely chopped fresh parsley
1	cup mayonnaise
1	teaspoon lemon juice
	salt and pepper

Drain the oysters and discard liquor. Combine eggs, milk, seafood seasoning, salt, and pepper. Combine bread crumbs and flour. Roll oysters in crumb mixture, then dip in egg mixture and roll in crumbs again. Fry in hot oil at moderate heat until golden brown on one side, about 2½ minutes. Turn carefully and brown the other side. Drain on absorbent paper. Serve with lemon wedges and tartar sauce.

Serves 6.

Tartar Sauce: Mix together the capers, pickles, parsley, mayonnaise, lemon juice, and salt and pepper to taste.

Chesapeake Appreciation Days was an annual wintertime event that celebrated the Bay and its most cherished catch: oysters. The downfall of this Bay tradition came when, year after year, it rained crabs and dogs when the event was held.

63

QUICK AND EASY FRIED OYSTERS

 *One good thing about Chesapeake cooking is that most of it is quick and easy. This recipe is too, but the addition of sweet and sour sauce, which can be made ahead of time, is a little unusual. I don't make the sauce every time I fry oysters, but there are times when you're looking for something a little different. My collection of oyster sauces, spanning many cultures and cooking styles, offers something for everyone.*

1–2   **cups dry pancake mix**
1   **pint oysters, drained**
    peanut oil for frying

SWEET AND SOUR SAUCE
½   **cup ketchup**
½   **cup orange marmalade**
3   **tablespoons red wine vinegar**
1   **tablespoon soy sauce**
    juice of 1 medium lemon or lime
½   **tablespoon dry mustard**
1   **teaspoon grated horseradish**
    dash cayenne pepper

Oysters: Drain oysters. Put pancake mix into a large, shallow bowl. Add oysters, a few at a time, and toss lightly until well coated. Shake off excess mix in a wire basket. Heat peanut oil to 350° F., and fry oysters until golden brown, 1½ to 2 minutes. Drain on absorbent paper. Repeat process until all oysters are cooked. Serve with Sweet and Sour Sauce.

Sweet and Sour Sauce: Mix all ingredients in a small saucepan. Heat, but do not boil, stirring constantly. Correct seasonings. Serve warm.
  Serves 4.

I look at a menu board like this and think of that notable oyster eater, the Roman emperor Vitellius, who reportedly once ate a thousand oysters at a single sitting. Do you think Mrs. Vitellius got much sleep that night? I doubt it!

CRUSTY COUNTRY FRIED OYSTERS

Oysters, pearls of the Bay, take on a special flavor when prepared with this wonderful recipe, my all-time favorite. Once you try them, it will be yours, too.

OYSTERS

- 2 eggs, beaten
- 3 tablespoons cold water
- 1 pint oysters, drained
- 1½ cups saltine cracker crumbs
  vegetable oil for frying

*"So if you go for oysters, and I go for ersters,
I'll order oysters, and cancel the ersters,
Oysters, ersters. Ersters, oysters.
Let's call the whole thing off!"*

—GEORGE AND IRA GERSHWIN, "LET'S CALL THE WHOLE THING OFF"

TARTAR SAUCE

- 1 cup mayonnaise
- 3 tablespoons minced sweet pickles
- 1 shallot, minced
- 2 tablespoons snipped fresh chives
- 2 tablespoons minced fresh parsley
- 1 tablespoon minced fresh tarragon
- 1 tablespoon capers
  Dijon mustard
  white wine vinegar

Oysters: Combine eggs and water. Dip oysters in the egg mixture and roll them in cracker crumbs. Heat oil to 375° F and fry oysters for about 2 minutes on each side, or until golden brown. Drain on absorbent paper. Serve with Tartar Sauce.

Serves 4.

Tartar Sauce: Combine all ingredients and refrigerate to blend flavors.

Photograph by Marion E. warren.

OYSTER AND CRAB FRITTERS

This is a delightful recipe that combines two of my favorite foods and two separate methods of preparation. If you choose not to skillet-fry these, an alternative method is deep-frying. You'll get equally good, but different, results.

"Son, anybody can shuck an oyster. But not everybody can make a living at it."
— KIE TYLER AT
CRISFIELD, MARYLAND, 1999

Photograph by Bryan Hatchett.

FRITTERS

1	**pint oysters and liquor**
	corn flake crumbs
2	**eggs, separated**
½	**cup milk**
1	**teaspoon grated lemon zest**
¾	**cup all-purpose flour**
1	**teaspoon baking powder**
1	**teaspoon salt**
½	**pound crabmeat**
	vegetable oil for frying

CURRY SAUCE

1½	**cups dry white wine**
2	**tablespoons oyster liquor**
¼	**teaspoon curry powder**
1½	**tablespoons cornstarch**
3	**tablespoons cream**
	freshly ground white pepper

Fritters: Drain oysters, reserving 2 tablespoons oyster liquor for the sauce. Cut the oysters into quarters and roll them in corn flake crumbs. Make Curry Sauce (see below). Whisk the egg yolks, milk, and lemon zest in a bowl. Sift the flour, baking powder, and salt together and add them to the egg yolks, mixing well. Add the crab meat and stir. Add a pinch of salt to the egg whites and whip until stiff. Stir 2 tablespoons into the egg yolk batter; then fold in the remaining whites and the oysters.

Heat a skillet until a drop of water sizzles on the surface, and brush lightly with oil. Drop fritter mixture by the tablespoonful into the skillet. Turn once to brown both sides evenly. Serve immediately with the warm sauce.

Serves 6 to 8.

Curry Sauce: Simmer the wine, oyster liquor, and curry powder in an uncovered saucepan for 15 minutes. Combine the cornstarch and cream; add them to the wine mixture and heat, stirring constantly, until thick. Season to taste with pepper and keep sauce warm.

LOWER MACHODOC CREEK OYSTER FRITTERS

Serve these oyster fritters with a steaming bowl of oyster chowder for a hearty supper. This recipe honors my friends aboard First Lady.

1	**pint oysters and liquor**
½	**cup milk**
2	**eggs**
¾	**cup sifted all-purpose flour**
⅔	**cup saltine cracker crumbs**
1¼	**teaspoons baking powder**
1	**tablespoon chopped fresh parsley**
1	**teaspoon salt**
	freshly ground black pepper
	cayenne pepper
	peanut oil for deep frying
	lemon wedges
	tartar sauce

Drain oysters and reserve ½ cup liquor (add water to make ½ cup if necessary). Chop the oysters and set aside. Combine the oyster liquor, milk, and eggs in a bowl; beat thoroughly with a whisk. Add flour and beat until smooth. Add cracker crumbs, baking powder, and parsley and mix well. Add the oysters, salt, black pepper, and cayenne pepper to taste. Allow to rest and thicken for 15 minutes before frying.

In a deep saucepan, heat the oil to 365°F. Drop fritters by the spoonful into the oil and fry until light golden brown on one side. Then turn them gently and brown on the other. Drain on absorbent paper and serve at once with lemon wedges and tartar sauce.

Look at it this way: For ten bucks, you can have two orders of oyster fritters or six hotdogs and a cold drink. I know what I'm having. Do you? Hint: It rhymes with "royster-jitters."

OYSTER-POTATO WRAP

 A crisp potato coating adds flavor and texture to oysters served as an appetizer or supper entrée.

¼ **cup all-purpose flour**
½ **teaspoon salt**
½ **teaspoon seafood seasoning**
¼ **cup sour cream**
1 **egg, beaten**
2 **cups finely shredded potatoes, drained**
1 **pint oysters, well drained**
oil for deep frying

Mix the flour, salt and seafood seasoning in a small bowl. Add the sour cream and mix well. Combine this mixture with the beaten egg. Add the potatoes and blend thoroughly. Add 4 or 5 oysters at a time to this mixture.

In a deep saucepan, heat the oil to 365°F. Drop fritters by tablespoonfuls into the oil, making sure to have an oyster in each spoonful. Do not crowd them; they should be free to float one layer deep. Fry 2 to 3 minutes, or until golden brown. Drain on absorbent paper.
Serves 4.

When I see a sign that reads "Oyster Sandwich," why, my eyes water with joy and I begin to feel faint. Of course, I have to pull over and order one. My ex-wives didn't believe me when I arrived home late after these frequent pit stops. Maybe that explains why they're ex-wives.

DENTON'S OYSTER HOUSE FRIED OYSTERS

These flavorful oyster appetizers are accented with the light and buttery texture of puff pastry. Topped with an elegant oyster purée, they can be served with fresh, dry martinis for the perfect cocktail party combination.

1   **pint oysters and liquor**
¾   **cup beer**
1   **egg**
2   **tablespoons peanut oil**
1   **cup cornstarch**
1   **tablespoon chopped scallion, green part only**
   salt and freshly ground black pepper
   peanut oil for frying
   cornstarch for dredging

Drain the oysters and set them aside.. Discard the liquor. Combine the beer, egg, oil, and cornstarch. Whip to a smooth batter, stir in the scallions, and season to taste with salt and pepper.

Pour 3 inches of peanut oil into a deep-sided heavy pot and heat to 360°F. Dredge the oysters lightly in cornstarch, and then dip them in the batter, coating only as many at one time as you can fry in one batch. Do not crowd the pot or the oysters will stick together. Fry a few at a time in the hot oil. Drain on paper towels and serve hot.

Serves 4.

When I first saw this sign, I said "Wow, a new way to enjoy Bay oysters. Scooping them right off the reefs and into your mouth from the comfort of an oyster boat!" As it turned out, the reference wasn't to an actual floating boat, but to the cardboard containers in which the oysters were served. Darn.

OYSTERS IN BEER BATTER

This lightly done batter can be adjusted to suit your palate: If you like your batter a little heavier, using less liquid is okay. If you like it lighter—and if you don't have enough oyster liquor—you can add a couple of tablespoonfuls of bottled clam juice and adjust the salt.

1	**pint oysters and liquor**
2	**tablespoons butter**
2	**eggs**
⅔	**cup beer**
	1 cup all-purpose flour
1	**cup oyster liquor**
¼	**teaspoon salt**
¼	**teaspoon paprika**
	dash of Tabasco sauce
	peanut oil for deep frying

GARLIC MAYONNAISE

6	**cloves garlic, peeled**
3	**egg yolks**
2	**tablespoon light olive oil**
	salt and freshly ground black pepper

Drain oysters, reserving liquor, and pat dry. Melt the butter. Beat the eggs lightly and combine with the beer, flour, salt, paprika, Tabasco sauce and melted butter. Stir until the mixture is smooth. Heat the oil to 375°F and deep fry the oysters for 3 to 4 minutes. Serve with Garlic Mayonnaise.

Garlic Mayonnaise: Mince garlic in a food processor. Add egg yolk and process until smooth. Slowly drizzle in the olive oil until it's all incorporated. Then season to taste with salt and pepper.
Serves 4.

Folks always ask, "What do you drink while slurping oysters?" Well, generally, I'll drink whatever is suitable and on hand. My favorite libations with oysters are beer, ice-cold champagne and equally ice-cold Chardonnay, and not necessarily in that order. Sometimes I'll even pair bivalves with a cup of Chesapeake hard cider.

DEALE OVEN FRIED OYSTERS

This one is for the purists who like their oysters unadorned—and I love them this way. Here, the oyster is the dish, so it's essential to use freshly shucked oysters for the ultimate in flavor. Your guests are going to love them, and they'll love you, too.

1 **quart oysters and liquor**
2 **eggs**
1 **cup saltine cracker crumbs**

Preheat oven to 400°F. Drain the oysters and discard the liquor. Dip the oysters in beaten egg. Roll in cracker crumbs. place on a lightly greased broiler rack and cook 15 to 20 minutes.
Serves 6.

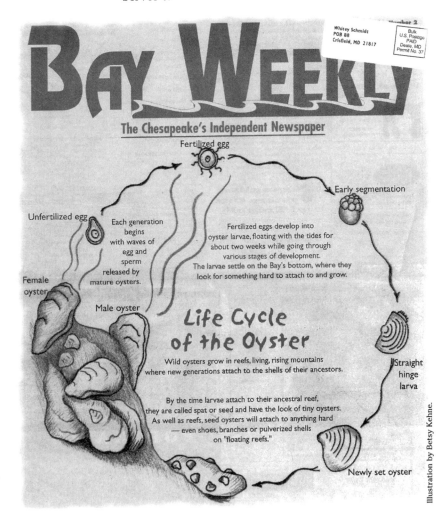

Illustration by Betsy Kehne.

*L**ife Cycle of the Oyster:***
Each generation begins with waves of eggs and sperm released by mature oysters. Fertilized eggs develop into oyster larvae, floating with the tides for about two weeks while going through progressive states of development. In the wild, the larvae settle to the Bay's bottom, where they look for something hard to attach to and grow.

71

THE VIRGINIAN SEA OYSTER PLATTER

You can substitute other types of fish into this dish depending on the season and the catch. I like to add a few large shrimp, too. But don't be tempted to leave out the oysters: They enhance this platter to such a degree that it will make you famous among your guests and, quite possibly, your countrymen.

 1   **cup all-purpose flour**
     pinch of cayenne pepper
     salt and pepper
 ½ **cup milk**
     dash of Tabasco sauce
 1   **cup fine yellow cornmeal**
 1½ **pounds rockfish filets**
 ½ **pint oysters and liquor**
     peanut oil for deep frying
 1   **large onion, cut into very thin rings**

DIPPING SAUCE
 3   **cups mayonnaise**
 ⅓ **cup minced green onion**
 3   **tablespoons drained capers**
 1   **tablespoon Worcestershire sauce**
 1   **tablespoon prepared horseradish**

 1   **tablespoon finely chopped parsley**
 1   **clove garlic, crushed**
     a few drops of Tabasco sauce

Combine the flour, cayenne pepper, salt, and pepper in a shallow dish and stir to mix. In another shallow dish, combine the milk and Tabasco sauce. Put the cornmeal in a third shallow dish. Cut each rockfish filet into 2 to 4 even pieces. Drain the oysters and fish on absorbent paper and pat dry.

Heat 2 inches of oil to 375°F in a deep fryer. Toss the sliced onion in the seasoned flour, separating the rings, and thoroughly coating. Shake off excess flour and add the onions to the hot fat. Fry until crisp and brown, 1 to 2 minutes. Drain on absorbent paper and keep warm in a low oven.

Dust the rockfish pieces with seasoned flour, shaking off excess. Dip them in the milk, allowing excess to drip off, and then thoroughly coat them with cornmeal. Shake off excess and add the fish to the hot oil. Fry, turning once or twice, until golden and crisp, 5 to 7 minutes. Drain on absorbent paper and keep warm in the oven. Repeat with the oysters, frying them 2 to 3 minutes.

Arrange the fish and oysters on a large platter, pile the onions on top, and pass the dipping sauce.

Serves 4.

Dipping Sauce: Combine all ingredients in a large bowl. Mix well and store in a covered container in the refrigerator. Serve with hot or cold cooked shrimp or other seafood.

Makes about 3 cups. Refrigerate any leftover sauce.

*Y*ou *wonder if this sign was made by Bond . . . James Bond, himself an oyster fan of great renown.*

MARYLAND HOUSE CORNMEAL FRIED OYSTERS

You can add a nice side of crisp coleslaw to make this meal an "event." I like to include a basket of fresh bread or rolls, pitchers of ice water, bottles of ice-cold beer and decanters of Chardonnay on ice to round out the effect.

   1   **cup cornmeal**
  ½   **teaspoon salt**
  ½   **teaspoon freshly ground black pepper**
  ½   **teaspoon cayenne pepper**
   1   **pint oysters and liquor**
        peanut oil for deep frying

TARTAR SAUCE
  1-2   **teaspoons minced onion**
  1½–2 **tablespoons chopped sweet pickle**
  1–2   **tablespoons chopped green olives**
   ¾   **cup mayonnaise**

In a large bowl, season the cornmeal with the salt, black pepper, and cayenne pepper. Drain oysters, and roll each one in the cornmeal mixture until covered. Shake off any excess. Heat oil to 360°F and fry until golden brown, about 2 minutes. Drain on absorbent paper and serve with Tartar sauce.
    Serves 4.

Tartar Sauce: Combine all ingredients. Store in a covered jar in the refrigerator.
    Makes about 1 cup.

When I saw this sign it made my stomach rumble. I began with a crab cake, followed by fried oysters, and topped it off with an Italian sausage smothered with plenty of fried onions. I quit there. Burp. Thanks.

BIG VIN'S OYSTER FRITTERS

Award-winning photographer Vince Lupo has contributed many photos throughout this book. Here is one of Big Vin's favorite recipes for fritters. As this Toronto native says: "You can't get these in Canada, Baby."

1   **pint oysters and liquor**
2   **cups all-purpose flour**
1   **tablespoon baking powder**
1   **teaspoon salt**
2   **eggs, beaten**
1   **cup milk**
1   **tablespoon melted butter**
    peanut oil for frying

Drain oysters and chop them. Discard the oyster liquor In a large bowl, combine flour, baking powder, and salt. In a small bowl, combine eggs, milk, and butter. Pour into dry ingredients and stir until smooth. Add oysters. Heat oil to 360°F. Drop batter by the teaspoonful into hot oil and fry until golden brown, about 3 minutes. Drain on absorbent paper.

Serves 6.

The forms taken by oyster art are myriad. This time, it's in the form of a carry-out container used for fried or frittered oysters. Talk about art mirroring life!

OYSTER LOAF WITH BLUE CHEESE CRUMBLE

In New Orleans, the Oyster Po' Boy is called "The Peacemaker." As the story goes, the husband who had been out carousing all night long brought one of these oversized sandwiches home to his waiting—and angry—wife, who of course forgave all with the first mouthful. I tried this with my last two wives but it didn't work. Maybe that's because I had eaten half the oyster loaf on the way home?

1   **cup yellow cornmeal**
½   **teaspoon salt**
½   **teaspoon freshly ground black pepper**
½   **teaspoon cayenne pepper**
1   **pint oysters, drained**
    peanut oil for frying
1   **loaf fresh French bread**
    butter
    juice of ½ lemon

½   **cup crumbled blue cheese,**
    plus additional for serving
4   **sprigs fresh parsley**

In a large bowl, season the cornmeal with the salt, black pepper, and cayenne pepper, and roll each oyster in the mixture until covered. Heat oil to 360°F and fry until golden brown, about 2 minutes. Drain on paper towels.

To make oyster loaf, slice the French bread lengthwise and butter the cut sides generously. Toast lightly in a hot oven and mound with fried oysters. Sprinkle with lemon juice and blue cheese. Bake at 450°F until golden and cheese begins to melt. Serve on a platter topped with sprigs of parsley and additional blue cheese.

Serves 4.

There's nothing better with my oyster loaf than a bowl of killer crab soup and a tall glass of freshly squeezed lemonade.

OYSTERS NATHAN

My dear friend and fellow bon vivant, Nate Livingston, devised this piquant sauce in his Bay country kitchen overlooking the Magothy River. I think you'll agree that Nate is a sous-chef par excellence—to say nothing of his pool-shooting prowess.

SPICY MUSTARD SAUCE

- ½ **cup heavy cream**
- ¼ **cup mayonnaise**
- 1 **tablespoon Porter and Spicy brown mustard**
- 1 **teaspoon minced fresh chives**
- 1 **teaspoon minced fresh parsley pinch of salt**

OYSTERS

- 1 **pint oysters and liquor**
- ½ **cup milk**
- 1 **cup yellow cornmeal vegetable oil for frying**

Spicy Mustard Sauce: Whip the cream until stiff peaks form. In a separate bowl, combine the mayonnaise, mustard, chives, parsley and salt. Carefully fold the mayonnaise mixture into the whipped cream just until all the ingredients are combined. Refrigerate until needed.

Oysters: Drain the oysters and discard the oyster liquor. Dip the oysters into the milk and then into cornmeal. Shake gently to remove excess cornmeal. Heat a large frying pan over medium heat and then add the vegetable oil. When the oil is hot, carefully add the oysters and cook until golden brown, 3 to 4 minutes per side. Drain on absorbent paper.

Put a generous dollop of the sauce in the center of each plate and arrange the oysters around it. Serve while the oysters are hot.

Serves 4.

You'll notice that many seafood restaurants and markets still display "Oysters R in Season" signs, which traditionally meant that oysters were available only during the months that have the letter R in their names. But rest assured, thanks to the wonders of modern shipping methods, they can be eaten year round, 'round the world.

CHAPTER 4
Oh, My . . .
Oyster Pie!

REVELL'S NECK OYSTER PIE

Once emptied of their succulent Chesapeake Bay treasures, oyster cans were often discarded or used to hold old paintbrushes. In 2002, the Chesapeake Bay Maritime Museum in St. Michaels, Maryland, acquired more than 600 antique oyster cans, dating from the 1880s, elevating them to their rightful place—history by the gallon.

On Maryland's Eastern Shore, no Thanksgiving dinner is complete without an oyster pie. I suggest you wait until the very last minute to put this one in the oven. When it's done, serve it right from the dish. Your guests will indeed be inclined to sigh: "Oh, my . . . oyster pie."

2	unbaked 9-inch pie crusts
4	tablespoons bacon drippings
1	cup chopped celery
½	cup chopped fresh parsley
2	medium onions, chopped
1	medium green pepper, chopped
3	tablespoons all-purpose flour
2	quarts oysters
1	tablespoon Worcestershire sauce
½	teaspoon salt
¼	teaspoon Tabasco sauce
	freshly grated nutmeg

In the bacon drippings, sauté the celery, parsley, onions, and green pepper until they are soft. Sprinkle the flour into the mixture and stir until well blended. Add the oysters, Worcestershire sauce, salt, and Tabasco sauce and let simmer for 10 minutes. Pour the mixture into a deep dish casserole lined with a pastry crust. Cover with the second crust, crimp edges, and cut slits in the top crust with a sharp knife. Sprinkle with nutmeg and bake at 325°F for 45 minutes.

Serves 8.

QUAKER NECK LANDING OYSTER SOUFFLÉ

Soufflés are easier to make than you might think, but be sure to bring the dish straight from the oven to the table or your masterpiece will collapse before it's appreciated. This savory oyster dish, once it makes it there, will jump off the table.

1	**pint oysters and liquor**
4	**tablespoons butter, divided**
3	**tablespoons all-purpose flour**
½	**cup warm half-and-half**
½	**teaspoon salt**
½	**teaspoon white pepper**
	pinch of seafood seasoning
3	**eggs, separated**

Drain the oysters and reserve ½ cup of the liquor. Pat the oysters dry with paper towels. Melt 3 tablespoons of the butter in a saucepan. (Allow the other tablespoon to soften.) Add the flour to the butter in the saucepan and mix well. Mix the ½ cup of oyster liquor with the half-and-half and slowly stir into the butter and flour. Continue cooking over low heat, stirring constantly, until the sauce is thickened and smooth.

Remove from heat and mix the oysters into the sauce. Season with salt, white pepper, and seafood seasoning. Beat the egg yolks well and stir them into the oyster mixture. Let the oyster mixture cool for 2 to 3 minutes.

Grease the sides and bottom of a 7-inch ovenproof soufflé dish with the remaining tablespoon of butter.

Beat the egg whites until stiff, but not dry, and peaks form. Fold the egg whites carefully into the oyster mixture. Pour the mixture into the soufflé dish and bake for 30 to 35 minutes at 325°F or until firm.

Serve immediately.

Serves 6.

You never know when the urge will strike. A couple of years ago I was driving north on I-95 and took a cut-off from Route 17. It was a winding country road and I wasn't thinking about oysters—honest. Then I saw this sign hanging from a tree and snapped the photo. Suddenly, something snapped in my mind, too: I wouldn't be happy until I had another oyster fix.

INDIAN CREEK OYSTER PIE

Pies contribute much to good eating. They can convey the flavors of meat, chicken and, of course, fruit with such panache. A pie doesn't have to have a top crust; this one doesn't. However, if you're inclined to add one, try topping the pie with mashed potatoes before baking.

> 8   **tablespoons butter, divided**
> 2   **quarts oysters and liquor**
> 4   **green onions, sliced**
> 1½   **cups white button mushrooms, quartered**
> 1   **teaspoon Worcestershire sauce**
>   **a few dashes of Tabasco sauce**
> 4   **cups coarsely crushed saltine crackers**
> 2   **tablespoons chopped parsley**
> 3   **tablespoons half-and-half**

Butter a 3-quart rectangular baking dish and set it aside. Drain the oysters well, reserving 3 tablespoons of the oyster liquor. Set the oysters and liquor aside.

In a large skillet, cook the green onions and the mushrooms in 2 tablespoons of the butter until tender. Cool slightly. Add the drained oysters, Worcestershire sauce, and Tabasco sauce; set this mixture aside.

Melt the remaining 6 tablespoons of butter. In a bowl, combine the crushed saltines, melted butter, and parsley; set this mixture aside. Combine the reserved oyster liquor with the half-and-half and set aside.

Sprinkle about 1 cup of the crumb mixture in the bottom of the baking dish. Top with half the oyster and mushroom mixture and half the remaining crumb mixture, and drizzle with half the oyster liquor mixture. Add the rest of the oyster and mushroom mixture and the rest of the crumb mixture, and drizzle with the rest of the oyster liquor mixture.

Bake, uncovered, at 425°F for 30 to 35 minutes or until the oysters in the center of the dish curl around the edges.

Serves 12.

Life on the Chesapeake Bay is divided into two seasons: when crabs are here and when oysters are here. This photo shows some local product during a recent season when oysters, blessedly, were here.

KEDGE'S STRAIT OYSTER CRÊPES

 The secret ingredient in these do-ahead crêpes is Fontina cheese. It is one of Italy's great cheeses. Semi-firm yet creamy, Fontina has a mild, nutty flavor, and the fact that it melts easily and smoothly makes it perfect for these oyster crêpes.

1	**quart oysters and liquor**
3	**cups chicken stock**
1	**bunch broccoli**
	salt and freshly ground pepper
2	**sticks butter plus additional for greasing baking dish**
½	**cup all-purpose flour**
	pinch of cayenne pepper
⅓	**cup dry vermouth**
1	**pint heavy cream, divided**
1½	**cups freshly grated fontina cheese, divided**
24	**7-inch crêpes**
3	**tablespoons capers**

Drain the oysters, reserving ⅔ cup of the liquor, and place them in a large bowl. Warm the liquor and chicken stock in a saucepan.

Wash, peel, and blanch the broccoli in boiling water. Refresh in cold water, drain, and chop into ¼-inch pieces.

Melt 4 tablespoons of the butter in a large pan and toss the broccoli until it is well coated. Season with pepper, remove it with a slotted spoon, and set aside in the bowl with the oysters.

If you like to buy the freshest seafood every time, I suggest you get to know your local fishmonger. Go back again and again until you forge a personal relationship with him, like I've done with the fine folks at Linton's, my local seafood place here in Crisfield. They'll take good care of you, especially if you show an interest in their expertise.

Melt the remaining butter, stir in the flour, salt, and cayenne pepper, and cook until bubbling. Remove from the heat and whisk in the stock. Return to the heat and boil, stirring constantly, until the sauce thickens. Add the vermouth and ½ cup of the heavy cream, and simmer for 10 minutes.

Stir enough of the sauce into the oysters and broccoli to bind them. Adjust the seasonings.

Mix the remaining cream and 1 cup of the cheese. Spread this mixture on the bottom of a large, shallow, buttered baking dish. Fill each crêpe with about 2 tablespoons of the oyster mixture; roll crêpes and arrange them in one layer, seam side down, in the dish. Add the capers to the sauce, pour it over the crêpes, and top with the remaining cheese.

Cover with foil, bake at 350°F for 30 minutes, and serve immediately.

Serves 12.

81

STEWART NECK ROCKEFELLER POTPIE

A touch of nutmeg enlivens both the spinach and the fresh seafood in this delicate potpie. The dish can be prepared well in advance and popped into the oven when your guests arrive.

SPINACH

- 2 tablespoons butter
- 2 packages (10-ounces each) frozen chopped spinach, drained and squeezed dry
- 1 teaspoon salt
- ½ teaspoon freshly ground black pepper pinch of freshly grated nutmeg

SEAFOOD

- 1 pound mixed seafood of your choice (shrimp, flounder, clams, crabmeat, oysters)
- ½ cup white wine
- 2 tablespoons butter
- 2 tablespoons all-purpose flour
- 1½ cups milk
- 1 cup freshly grated Gruyère cheese

Spinach: In a sauté pan, heat the butter, add the spinach, and sauté just until softened and heated through. Season with salt, pepper and nutmeg. Spread in an ovenproof baking dish.

Seafood: Place the seafood in a sauté pan and add the wine. Simmer until the seafood is cooked through, about 2 to 3 minutes. Drain, reserving ¼ cup of the the poaching liquid. Set the seafood aside.

In another saucepan, melt the butter, add the flour, and cook until white bubbles begin to form. Whisk in the reserved poaching liquid and the milk, stirring until the sauce is thick and smooth. Stir in the cheese and set aside.

Assembly: Cut the seafood into bite-size chunks and spread it over the spinach. Top with the sauce and bake at 400°F until the sauce bubbles. Serve at once.

Serves 4.

My friend Larry Antonik discovered these 8-inch oyster shells near Cedar Island, off Virginia's lower Eastern Shore. Unfortunately, the succulent giants that once inhabited these shells were gone. Larry, are you the guilty party?

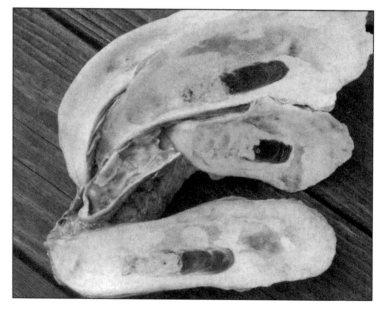

OYSTERSHELL POINT OYSTER PIE

"Substantial" and "savory" best describe the "main course" pies about which Bay country folks justifiably boast. This dish has caused spontaneous dancing among my Crab Lab taste testers. I also use it as a hearty side dish. So do many friends, to ravenous reviews.

	butter for greasing pan
36	oysters in shells
8	slices bacon
1	tablespoon oil
1	large onion, chopped
3	cups sliced mushrooms
1	red bell pepper, chopped
½	cup all-purpose flour
	pinch of salt
	pinch of cayenne pepper
¼	cup chopped fresh parsley
8	ounces puff pastry, thawed

Butter a deep pie pan. Shuck the oysters, reserving the liquor and discarding the shells. Pat the oysters dry.

Heat the bacon in a skillet until the fat runs; then raise the heat and fry until crispy. Remove from the pan, chop roughly, and set aside.

Add the oil to the bacon drippings remaining in the pan and heat. When hot, add the onion, mushrooms, and bell pepper. Toss to coat, then cover the pan and simmer the vegetables for about 5 minutes. Stir in the flour, with salt and cayenne pepper to taste, and add the reserved oyster liquor. After a few turns with a wooden spoon, fold in the oysters, bacon, and parsley.

Place the ingredients into the pie pan. Roll out the puff pastry on a lightly floured surface and cover the pie with it. Cut a cross in the top to let the steam escape. Bake at 400°F for 20 to 25 minutes or until puffy and golden.

Serves 6.

Did you know that Dooley's Prong—an estuary of Piccowaxen Creek off the Potomac River—was the site of the largest Indian oyster-shell field on the Bay? Beginning at this creek and running south for two miles, shell depths vary from 1 to 4 feet, with widths of up to 300 feet.

BACK WYE SEAFOOD PIE

Who doesn't love Eggs Benedict for brunch? I know I do. I created this one on the fly when friends called while on the road to announce they were dropping in for a visit. I guess cell phones do have a purpose.

CRAB CAKE CRUST

1	**pound lump crabmeat**
½	**cup 2-day-old hamburger bun crumbs**
1	**teaspoon seafood seasoning**
1	**heaping tablespoon mayonnaise**
1	**tablespoon Worcestershire sauce**
2	**tablespoons butter**
1	**tablespoon peanut oil**

PIE

6	**English muffins**
6	**eggs**
1¼	**cups heavy cream**
¼	**cup all-purpose flour**
½	**cup mayonnaise**
¼	**cup chopped green onions**
2	**tablespoons freshly squeezed lemon juice**
1	**teaspoon salt**
¼	**teaspoon cayenne pepper**
1	**pint oysters, drained and chopped**
2	**tablespoons melted butter**

Crab Cake Crust: In a mixing bowl, gently combine the crabmeat, hamburger bun crumbs, seafood seasoning, mayonnaise, and Worcestershire sauce. Form the mixture into 6 cakes. Cover and refrigerate for half an hour.

Heat the butter with the peanut oil and sauté the crab cakes until golden, about 3 minutes on each side. Drain on paper towels. Refrigerate the cooked crab cakes until it's time to bake the pie.

Pie: Spray an ovenproof baking dish with nonstick cooking spray. Split the English muffins and place half of them in the bottom of the baking dish.

In a large mixing bowl, whisk together the eggs, cream, flour, mayonnaise, green onions, lemon juice, salt, and cayenne pepper. Pour the egg mixture over the English muffins. Add the oysters and set the remaining muffins on top. Cover the baking dish and refrigerate it overnight.

Assembly: When ready to serve, remove the baking dish and cooked crab cakes from the refrigerator and allow them to sit at room temperature for 30 minutes. Top each English muffin with a crab cake. Brush the tops with the melted butter, and bake at 375° for 30 to 40 minutes, until puffed and golden.

Serves 6.

Nothing stimulates the appetite like a table full of oysters on the half-shell. Does this sight affect you like it does me?

CHINCOTEAGUE ISLAND OYSTER PIE

"In Oyster days, there is nothing to Fear;
Taste on the first you are good for a Year.
They cure every ill, they are all that is good;
They are excellent cold, escalloped, or stew'd.
But if chance the first day puts them out of your power
Eat double the quantity every hour;
The effect will assuredly prove near the same,
And cure every ill that the Doctors can name."

—J.L. MARKS, 1827

1 **pint oysters and liquor**
1 **large onion, thinly sliced**
4 **small potatoes, peeled and thinly sliced**
2 **large bay leaves**
½ **teaspoon salt**
generous sprinkling of freshly ground black pepper
pinch of cayenne pepper
½ **cup warm half-and-half**
1 **unbaked 8- or 9-inch pie crust**

Drain oysters, reserving 2 tablespoons of the oyster liquor. Boil potato and onion slices in a little water until softenend but not cooked through. Arrange alternate layers of oysters, onion slices, and potato slices in an 8- or 9-inch pie pan.

Place the bay leaves in the center of the pie and season the pie with salt, black pepper, and cayenne pepper.

Mix the reserved 2 tablespoons of oyster liquor with the half-and-half and pour the mixture over the top of the pie.

Cover with the pie crust and crimp the edges around the pie pan. Prick the dough in several places with a fork. Bake at 450°F for approximately 15 minutes until crust is golden brown. Remove bay leaves and serve immediately.

Serves 6.

Chincoteague Island is one of my favorite spots to visit, be it for a day, a week or even a year. I eat the local seafood till my mind is clear, and wash it all down with a cold glass of beer.

Tonytank Creek Oyster-Bacon Quiche

Originally, quiches were made with heavy cream and no cheese. As the dish has evolved, cheese has become a standard ingredient. While I suggest cheddar with this dish, it's really your choice. Some cheeses you might try are Gruyère, Swiss, or Emmentaler.

8	slices bacon
1	pint oysters, poached in their own liquor
4	eggs
½	cup heavy whipping cream
1	cup milk
1	tablespoon all-purpose flour
1½	cups grated cheddar cheese
1	teaspoon salt
½	teaspoon freshly ground black pepper
½	teaspoon seafood seasoning
1	teaspoon Tabasco sauce
1	unbaked 10-inch pie crust
	chopped fresh parsley

In a large pan over medium heat, sauté the bacon until crisp, drain it on paper towels, and crumble it.

Drain the poached oysters, reserving ½ cup of the oyster liquor. In a medium bowl, combine the bacon and the oysters.

In another medium bowl, whisk together the eggs, cream, milk, flour, cheese, salt, pepper, seafood seasoning, Tabasco sauce, and reserved oyster liquor. Place the pie crust in a pie pan. Blend the oyster-bacon mixture into the egg mixture and pour into the pie shell. Bake at 350°F until set, about 25 minutes. Allow to cool before slicing into wedges. Garnish with parsley.

Serves 6.

Photograph by Vince Lupo.

Here the author and his friend Linda Meyer slurp oysters at Kinkead's in Washington, D.C. Boy, what a tough job!

OLD LINE OYSTER PIE

This classic oyster pie recipe was standardized by the Seafood Marketing Authority, Department of Economic and Community Development, Annapolis, Maryland. Thanks guys!

PIE

2   unbaked 9-inch pie crusts
2   cups peeled potatoes, slightly
       undercooked and then sliced
1   pint oysters and liquor
4   hard-cooked eggs, shelled and sliced
4   tablespoons margarine
    celery salt to taste
    lemon-and-pepper seasoning to taste

SAUCE

2   tablespoons margarine
2   tablespoons all-purpose flour
1   cup milk
    oyster liquor plus water to equal ½ cup
    salt and pepper

Pie: Place the bottom crust in a pie pan. Drain the potatoes well and place them on the crust. Remove the oysters from their container with a slotted spoon and arrange them over the potatoes, reserving the oyster liquor for the sauce. Arrange the egg slices over the oysters. Dot margarine over the top and sprinkle with celery salt and lemon-and-pepper seasoning.

Place the top crust on the pie, crimp the edges, and cut slits in the top. Bake at 400°F for 10 minutes; lower the heat to 375°F and bake until the crust is slightly browned, about 30 minutes. Let the pie stand for a few minutes before serving, and drain off any excess liquid.

Sauce: In a medium-size pan, melt the margarine and mix in the flour. Slowly add the milk, then the oyster liquor. Cook, stirring constantly, over medium heat until the mixture comes to a boil and thickens. Add salt and pepper to taste. Serve with the pie.

Serves 6.

"You come here for Chincoteague oysters, and we shell out."

Chief oyster shucker Marvin Johnson.

"Our full name is McGarvey's Saloon and Oyster Bar, and we serve up the succulent blighters in every which way. On the half shell, naturally, but also in pan roasts and chowders."

—TAKEN FROM ONE OF THE AUTHOR'S FAVORITE MENUS,
THE ONE AT MCGARVEY'S IN ANNAPOLIS

HOOPER'S ISLAND QUICHE

Ah, chives. This fragrant herb has slender, vivid green stems that are hollow. Their mild onion flavor adds a nice touch to this easy-to-assemble quiche. Can you imagine how wonderful the Crab Lab smells after we've cooked up one of these quiches?

1 **pint oysters and liquor**
3 **eggs**
6 **ounces cream cheese**
1½ **cups half-and-half**
2 **tablespoons all-purpose flour**
  pinch of nutmeg
  salt and freshly ground black pepper
1 **unbaked 10-inch pie crust, chilled**
½ **cup chopped chives**
½ **cup chopped parsley**

½ **cup sautéed chopped scallions**
1 **cup grated Swiss cheese**
¼ **cup grated Parmigiano-Reggiano cheese**
  additional chive stems for garnish

Drain the oysters and pat them dry. Strain and reserve ¼ cup of the oyster liquor. Beat the eggs in a bowl and blend in the softened cream cheese, oyster liquor, half-and-half, flour, nutmeg, and salt and pepper to taste.

Arrange the oysters on the chilled pastry shell and cover with the chives, parsley, scallions, and grated cheeses. Pour the egg mixture on top.

Bake at 375°F for about 45 minutes, until the custard is set and the top is golden brown; remove from the oven and cool for 5 minutes before serving. Garnish with chive stems.

Serves 6.

"Things go better with Coke." Especially if they're from the Bay and full of briny goodness, huh?

LONG POINT OYSTER PIE

Pine nuts are expensive, but there's a reason. They are found inside the pinecones themselves, which must be heated to remove the nuts. As expensive as they may be, pine nuts are worth the price. They add a delicate and flavorful richness to this marvelous oyster pie.

2	**bunches fresh spinach**
1	**small onion, finely chopped**
2	**cloves garlic, pressed**
1	**tablespoon unsalted butter**
2	**tablespoons olive oil**
1	**pint oysters and liquor**
2	**eggs**
¼	**cup half-and-half**
¼	**cup pine nuts, lightly toasted**
	salt and freshly ground black pepper
2	**unbaked 9-inch pie crusts**

Wash and chop the spinach and steam until soft. Cool and squeeze almost dry. Sauté the onion and garlic in butter and olive oil until they soften. Add the oysters.

Beat together the eggs and half-and-half and add to the onions and oysters. Add the spinach, pine nuts, and salt and pepper to taste. Blend well.

Roll out the bottom pie crust, place it in a 9-inch pie pan, and fill it with the oyster mixture. Cover with the top crust and crimp edges. Cut slits in the top crust to let steam out. Bake at 425°F for 10 minutes, then reduce heat to 375° and bake for 30 minutes or until pie is golden brown.

Serves 4 to 6.

Gloria Odend'hal (left) and Mary Riley see an oyster sign and just get in line. They don't even care what they're buying, exactly . . . just as long as it involves bivalves.

Photograph by Vince Lupo.

QUANTICO OYSTER PYE

The name of Quantico, a village on Maryland's Eastern Shore, comes from the Indian word that roughly translates into "dancing" or "place of dancing." Your guests will surely be dancing when they try this marvelous dish. It might even lead to the "Forbidden Dance" later on.

1 pint oysters and liquor
1 cup diced potatoes
½ cup sliced celery
4 tablespoons butter
5 tablespoons all-purpose flour
1 cup milk
1 teaspoon salt
  pinch of cayenne pepper
½ teaspoon Worcestershire sauce
1 can (8 ounces) peas and carrots, drained
1 unbaked 9-inch pie crust

In a saucepan, cook oysters in their liquor for about 5 minutes or until the edges begin to curl. Drain the oysters, reserving ½ cup of the oyster liquor.

Boil the potatoes in water until tender; drain. When they're cool, dice them.

In a 10-inch skillet, sauté the celery in the butter until tender. Blend in the flour and cook until bubbly. Stir in the oyster liquor and milk and cook, stirring constantly, until smooth and thick. Add the salt, cayenne pepper, Worcestershire sauce, peas and carrots, oysters, and potatoes and mix thoroughly. Pout into a 9-inch pie plate and top with pie crust. Cut slits in the top and bake at 425°F for 15 to 20 minutes or until crust is golden brown. Let stand for 10 minutes before serving.

Serves 6.

*S*hell Point, home of Graham and Bonita Bruce in Topping, Virginia, was once the site of the Adams Oyster House. The Bruces' house sits on 6 feet of oyster shell, hence the name.

CAPE CHARLES OYSTER AND SHRIMP PIE

 Are you looking for a Chesapeake-style seafood pie to serve with your entrées? Try this. Better yet, forget about the entrées. This one is a meal in itself. Bake a pie, pour some wine and enjoy.

1	**pint oysters and liquor**
½	**pound raw shrimp**
3	**tablespoons butter**
1	**small onion, chopped fine**
1	**cup chopped button mushrooms**
2	**tablespoons all-purpose flour**
½	**cup milk**
¾	**cup dry white wine**
1	**teaspoon salt**
½	**teaspoon paprika**
1	**unbaked 9-inch pie crust**

Drain oysters and reserve ¼ cup oyster liquor.

Peel and devein the shrimp and put them in salted boiling water to cover. As soon as the water comes to a boil again, remove the pan from the heat and drain the shrimp.

Melt the butter in a skillet and sauté the onion until soft. Add the mushrooms and flour and stir until the mixture is slighly thickened. Add milk, oyster liquor, wine and salt and cook for two minutes over medium heat, stirring contantly.

Butter a baking dish and pour in the sauce. Distribute the shrimp evenly over the sauce and the oysters over the shrimp. Sprinkle with paprika. Cover the dish with a thin layer of pie crust and make slits in it with a knife. Bake at 400°F until golden brown.

Serves 6.

Photograph by Pat Piper.

*T*his picture was taken by my friend Pat Piper at the Municipal Fish Wharf in southwest Washington, D.C. It's been a popular stopping-off spot of mine for over 50 years. I hope to return there soon. Thanks, Pat. It brings back fond memories.*

NANTICOKE OYSTER MUFFINS

Nanticoke has been associated with oystering for several generations. There used to be a steamboat wharf where skipjacks came to unload their catches. There's a bond between the three communities on the Wicomico County West Side—Nanticoke, Tyaskin, and Bivalve.

1	**pint oysters and liquor**
1¾	**cup chicken stock**
4	**tablespoons butter**
2	**tablespoons chopped onion**
1	**garlic clove, crushed**
3	**tablespoons all-purpose flour**
¼	**pound small mushrooms, sliced**
½	**cup diced cooked ham**
1	**tablespoon lemon juice**
	salt and freshly ground black pepper
4	**English muffins**
	lemon slices
	parsley sprigs

Drain the oysters and reserve ¼ cup of the liquor. Warm the liquor and chicken stock in a small saucepan.

Melt the butter in another saucepan and sauté the onion and garlic until tender. Discard the garlic. Stir in the flour and cook until bubbling. Remove from the heat and whisk in the hot chicken stock mixture. Return to the heat and boil, stirring constantly, until the mixture thickens. Then lower the heat and simmer for 3 minutes.

Stir in the mushrooms, ham, and lemon juice and boil for 1 minute. Add the oysters and cook until they begin to curl. Season with salt and pepper to taste.

Toast the English muffins and spoon the mixture over them. Garnish with lemon slices and parsley.

Serves 4.

Sure. Great. Happy New Year. Now please pass the Tabasco sauce.

HAPPY NEW YEAR
OYSTERS   SHRIMP
CLAMS   SALMON
SCALLOPS

INDIVIDUAL OYSTER PIES WICOMICO

Who could ever forget those individual, personal little pies that Mom used to make? Hot from the oven, they warmed my heart, too. This oyster-based version is almost as good as Mom's. Which is to say: They're as good as it gets.

- 6 tablespoons butter
- 1 cup sliced mushrooms
- 7 tablespoons all-purpose flour
- 1 teaspoon salt
- ½ teaspoon freshly grated nutmeg
- ½ teaspoon celery salt
  freshly ground black pepper
  pinch of cayenne pepper
- 3 cups milk
- 1 pint oysters and liquor
- 1 unbaked 8- or 9-inch pie crust

In a skillet, melt the butter and sauté the mushrooms for 2 minutes. Blend in the flour, salt, nutmeg, celery salt, and black pepper and cayenne pepper to taste. Then add the milk and simmer, stirring constantly, until thick and smooth.

Drain the oysters, reserving ½ cup of the liquor. Add the oysters and the reserved liquor to the mushroom mixture. Place this mixture in 4 individual baking dishes, cover each with a quarter of the pie crust, and make 2 or 3 slits in each crust. Bake at 450°F for about 10 minutes or until golden brown.

Serves 4.

Though each oyster-packing company carries a similar product, tags like this allow discerning wholesalers and consumers to pick their consistent favorites.

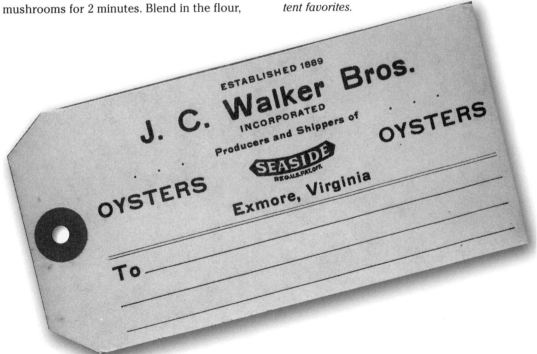

ANNEMESSEX OYSTER PIE

Country ham is the ingredient that brings the oysters in this recipe to their gustatory knees—that is, if they had any. The ham here has been dry-cured in a mixture of salt, sugar, and seasonings for several days. The salt is then rinsed off and the ham is slowly smoked over hardwood fires before being aged for 6 to 12 months.

     4   **tablespoons butter**
     4   **tablespoons all-purpose flour**
     1   **cup heavy cream**
         pinch of salt
     ½   **teaspoon dried onion flakes**
     ½   **teaspoon Worcestershire sauce**
     ¼   **teaspoon cayenne pepper**
     1   **cup chopped country ham**
     ½   **pint drained and chopped oysters**
     2   **unbaked 9-inch pie crusts**
         freshly grated nutmeg

In a saucepan, melt the butter. Add flour and cook until the mixture is smooth and golden.

Stir in the cream and cook until the sauce thickens. Add the salt, onion flakes, Worcestershire sauce, cayenne pepper, ham, and oysters. Continue to cook and stir for about 5 minutes.

Roll out the pie crusts and cut 10 circles 5 to 6 inches in diameter. Spread the oyster-and-ham mixture in the center of each circle and fold in half. Use a fork to press the edges together. Sprinkle each pie with nutmeg and bake at 425°F for 30 minutes or until the crust is golden brown.

Serves 6.

*I*t's getting so I can't drive down the highway without having to pull over! Oysters, clams, and decoys? Well, I suppose shellfish and decoys can go together! You can use the splinters to pick your teeth.

LORD'S GIFT OYSTER PYE

While baking any oyster pie, it's important to keep in mind that all ovens will cook at different rates, so always keep a careful eye on the crust. When it turns golden brown, the pie is done. Praise the Lord!

PIE

1	**pint oysters and liquor**
1½	**cups half-and-half**
8	**tablespoons butter, plus additional for greasing baking pan**
6	**tablespoons all-purpose flour**
3	**tablespoons Madeira**
	salt and freshly ground black pepper
6	**partially baked buttermilk biscuits (recipe below)**
	paprika

BUTTERMILK BISCUITS

2	**cups all-purpose flour**
3	**teaspoons baking powder**
1	**teaspoon salt**
¼	**cup butter**
¾	**cup buttermilk**

Pie: Drain the oysters and reserve ¼ cup of the oyster liquor. Warm the oyster liquor in a saucepan with the half-and-half.

Melt the butter in another saucepan, stir in the flour, and cook until bubbling. Remove from the heat and whisk in the warm liquids. Return to the heat, add the Madeira, and boil, stirring constantly, until the mixture thickens. Lower the heat and simmer for 3 minutes.

Stir in the oysters, season to taste with salt and pepper, and heat until the oysters curl. Pour the hot mixture into a buttered 1-quart casserole.

Biscuits: Stir together flour, baking powder, and salt in a mixing bowl. Cut in the butter with a pastry blender. Add the buttermilk and mix quickly. The dough should be soft and puffy but not sticky.

Turn the dough onto a floured counter and knead a few times. Pat out to about ½-inch thickness. (Do not make too thin.) Cut with a 3-inch cutter. Place them on an ungreased baking sheet and bake at 400°F for 5 minutes (they will not be done).

Arrange the partially cooked biscuits on top of the oyster mixture and sprinkle with paprika.

Bake at 425°F for about 10 minutes, or until the biscuits are completely baked and golden brown.

Serves 4.

There's only one thing to remember when serving a biscuit-crusted oyster pie like this: spoon some of the juices over the crust just before serving. Mmmm!

Photograph by Vince Lupo.

95

WINGATE POINT OYSTER PIE

Maybe it's the the colors—the bright red pimientos and the bright green peppers —in this delicate oyster pie that delight me at first. But it's the taste that keeps me coming back for more.

1	**pint oysters and liquor**
½	**cup diced celery**
½	**cup diced green pepper**
4	**tablespoons butter**
5	**tablespoons all-purpose flour**
1	**cup milk**
¾	**cup half-and-half**
½	**teaspoon seafood seasoning**
1	**teaspoon salt**
⅛	**teaspoon black pepper**
2	**tablespoons chopped pimientos**
1	**unbaked 9-inch pie crust**

In a saucepan, cook the oysters in their liquor for about 5 minutes, or until edges begin to curl. Drain. In another saucepan, cook celery and green pepper in butter until tender. Blend in flour and add milk and half-and-half. Cook until thick, stirring constantly.

Add oysters, seafood seasoning, salt, pepper, and pimientos. Pour into a casserole and top with pastry. Bake at 425°F for about 15 minutes, or until the crust is golden brown.

Serves 4.

Johnny Parks works the Chesapeake Bay year-round. When he's not selling his catch from this truck, he's making crab pots, carving decoys, shucking oysters, and delivering crabs. I'm glad to call him a buddy.

96

TANGIER ISLAND OYSTER PIE

Captain John Smith was the first European to lay eyes on Tangier Island. He did so in 1608. The island's name might have come from Smith's love for Tangier, in Africa. Or it might have come from the Indian word tanja, *which is derived from the small clay bowls the Indians made centuries ago. I wonder how many bowls of oysters were consumed back in those early days.*

1	**pint oysters and liquor**
6	**slices bacon**
2	**cups sliced fresh mushrooms**
½	**cup chopped onion**
½	**cup chopped green onion**
¼	**cup all-purpose flour**
½	**teaspoon salt**
¼	**teaspoon cayenne pepper**
¼	**cup chopped fresh parsley**
2	**tablespoons lemon juice**
1	**tablespoon butter, softened**
	biscuit topping (Bisquick® all-purpose baking mix)

Drain the oysters and dry them between sheets of absorbent paper. Discard the oyster liquor.

In a skillet, cook the bacon until crisp. Remove from pan, drain, crumble, and set aside. Reserve 3 tablespoons of the bacon fat.

Add the mushrooms, onion, and green onion to the bacon fat. Simmer for 5 minutes or until tender. Blend in flour, salt, and cayenne pepper. Stir in the oysters, bacon, parsley, and lemon juice.

Butter a 9-inch pie pan with the softened butter and turn the oyster mixture into the pan. Cover with biscuit topping and score to make a design. Bake at 400°F for 20 to 25 minutes or until biscuit topping is golden brown. Cut into wedges.

Serves 6.

Seafood markets are not just for fresh oysters; they're good spots to pick up an oyster knife, find a new brand of hot sauce, get some lemons or ice—or, when my Hotel Pontiac breaks down, a ride home. My local markets are also good for getting game scores and weather reports.

ROCKAWALKIN OYSTER-SPINACH PIE

Pecorino is the Italian term for any sheep's-milk cheese. Pecorino cheeses are similar to Parmesan: grainy, salty, nutty, hard, and delicious.

TOPPING

1½ cups Italian-style breadcrumbs
1 cup Pecorino-Romano cheese
2 tablespoons unsalted butter

FILLING

2 tablespoons unsalted butter
½ cup chopped onion
½ cup chopped celery
½ cup chopped green pepper
1 quart oysters, drained
½ teaspoons salt
½ teaspoon seafood seasoning
2 teaspoons freshly ground black pepper
1 cup heavy whipping cream
1 cup milk
8 ounces cream cheese at room temperature
1½ teaspoons Tabasco sauce
2 cups chopped fresh spinach
1 cup Pecorino-Romano cheese
3 eggs, beaten
2 unbaked 10-inch pie crusts

Topping: Put the breadcrumbs, cheese, and butter in a large bowl. Cut together with knives, as you would pie dough.

Filling: Melt the butter in a large pan. Add the onions, celery, and green peppers, and sauté over medium-high heat for 5 to 6 minutes, until the vegetables are soft.

Add the oysters, salt, seafood seasoning, pepper, cream, and milk and cook, stirring, until the oysters curl. Blend in the cream cheese and Tabasco sauce with a spoon, followed by the spinach, cheese, and eggs.

Place each pie crust in a pie pan. Divide the filling between the pans and bake at 350°F until set, about 25 minutes. Remove from the oven, sprinkle with topping, and return to the oven until just brown, about 35 minutes. Let cool to set before serving.

Serves 10.

One of my favorite forms of Chesapeake folk art is oyster cans. Here are some masterworks. Notice the eerily Elvis-looking man behind the wheel on the label of Christy's Oysters. While the King loved burnt bacon, peanut butter and medical-grade narcotics, I guess he also had a love for oysters. No wonder he could keep those hips shaking through the entirety of "Blue Hawaii."

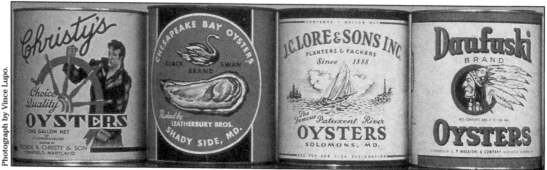

Photograph by Vince Lupo.

CHAPTER 5
The Royster with the Oyster
(A Festive Look at the Celebrated Oyster)

OYSTERS & MUSHROOMS AU GRATIN

ST. MARY'S COUNTY OYSTER FESTIVAL

First Annual Oyster Cook-Off

Saturday, October 18, 1980

ST. MARY'S COUNTY TECHNICAL CENTER
Leonardtown, Maryland

Au gratin dishes come in many forms, but they all share certain characteristics. Namely, they're covered with a crust—usually a combo of cheese and breadcrumbs—and put in a very hot oven or under the broiler to brown. This is one of my favorite au gratins.

1	pint oysters and liquor
2	tablespoons butter
2	tablespoons all-purpose flour
½	cup cream
½	teaspoon salt
½	teaspoon paprika
	pinch of seafood seasoning
1	can (4-ounce) sliced mushrooms, drained
1	teaspoon lemon juice
1	teaspoon Worcestershire sauce
	breadcrumbs for topping
	paprika for garnish
	ramekins for baking

Drain and dry oysters, reserving ½ cup of the liquor. Melt butter in a medium saucepan. Add flour and stir until blended. Slowly stir in the oyster liquor and cream. Add salt, paprika, and seafood seasoning. Cook, stirring, until mixture comes to a boil and thickens. Reduce heat and add mushrooms, lemon juice, Worcestershire sauce, and oysters. Heat, stirring, until the edges of the oysters just begin to curl. *Do not boil.* Spoon into ramekins and sprinkle with breadcrumbs and paprika. Place under broiler until golden brown, about 5 minutes. Serve immediately.

Serves 6.

If it's mid-October, it must be Oyster Festival time in St. Mary's County, Maryland. The first festival was held here on October 7, 1967. A little less than 1,000 visitors showed up. Attendance steadily grew over the years and in 1980 the first annual oyster cook-off was added. Today, more than 15,000 bivalve fans show up each year to consume oysters steamed, raw, scalded and fried. And I'm proud to call myself one of them (one of the bivalve fans, that is).

Oyster-Stuffed Sea Trout with Orange Sauce

Roystering is a term coined during the Victorian era for the raucous merriment that characterized festivities where oysters were served.

TROUT

24   oysters in shells
1   small carrot, finely diced
3   leeks (white part and ½ inch of the green), trimmed and cut
4   tablespoons butter
2   cups cooked brown rice
1   egg, beaten lightly
2   tablespoons fine dry breadcrumbs
¼   cup minced parsley
2   teaspoons grated orange rind
    salt and pepper
6   boneless whole trout, 12 ounces each
3   tablespoons melted butter
    juice of ½ lemon

ORANGE BUTTER

¼   cup dry white wine
2   tablespoons white wine vinegar
2   tablespoons finely chopped shallots
    juice of one orange
¼   teaspoon salt
    pinch of white pepper
½   pound butter, chilled and cut into small pieces

Trout: Shuck and drain oysters, discarding shells and liquor. In a skillet, cook carrot and leeks in butter over medium heat until tender, about 5 minutes. Remove from heat and stir in rice, oysters, egg, breadcrumbs, parsley, orange rind, and salt and pepper to taste. Set aside.

Fill the cavity of each trout with some of the stuffing and fold over. Arrange trout in a lightly buttered baking pan and brush with melted butter and lemon juice. Bake at 400°F for 20 to 25 minutes until skin is brown and crisp. Serve with Orange Butter.

Serves 6.

Orange Butter: In a small saucepan, combine wine, vinegar, shallots, orange juice, salt, and pepper. Reduce over high heat to 1 to 2 tablespoons. Remove pan from heat and whisk in several tablespoons butter, 1 tablespoon at a time. On the lowest possible heat, whisk in the remaining butter piece by piece. The butter must not melt, but form a creamy emulsion. When all of the butter is incorporated, turn off the heat and keep the sauce in a warm place until ready to use.

First oyster cooking contest entry blank.

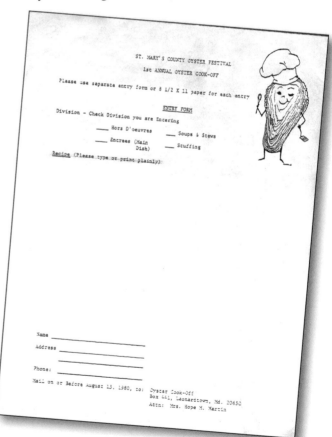

OLD SHUCKERS SCALLOPED OYSTERS

 *In earlier times, the old shuckers would have added some heavy cream to this dish and called it a chowder. Call it what you want, just call me before it's all gone.*

1   **quart oysters and liquor**
1   **stick butter**
2   **tablespoons finely chopped onion**
2   **cloves garlic, minced**
2   **tablespoons finely chopped green pepper**
2   **tablespoons all-purpose flour**
1¼ **cups cracker meal, divided**
1   **tablespoon lemon juice**
1   **tablespoon Worcestershire sauce salt and pepper to taste**

Heat oysters in their liquor until they curl. Melt the butter in a saucepan. Add the onion, green pepper, and garlic, and sauté until the onions soften. Add the flour and stir until it is golden brown. Add the oysters and liquor, 1 cup of the cracker meal, the lemon juice, Worcestershire sauce, and salt and pepper. Place in a 1½-quart baking dish and top with the remaining ¼ cup cracker meal. Bake at 375° for 15 to 20 minutes.

Serves 6.

For oyster-shucking tips, don't miss the chance to bend the experts' ears as they shuck their way to national glory each year at the U.S. National Oyster Shucking Championship, held in Leonardtown, Maryland. The male or female shuckers compete to represent the United States at the international championships held each year in Galway, Ireland.

St. James' Day Skewered Oysters

St. James' Day is July 25. Among large numbers of the poor, a superstition prevails that whoever eats oysters on that day will never be without money throughout the year.

36   oysters in shells
½   pound bacon, cut into 2-inch strips
½   teaspoon garlic powder
      tomato and onion wedges

Shuck and drain the oysters and discard shells and liquor. Wrap oysters in bacon strips. Using 10-inch skewers, alternate bacon-wrapped oysters with tomato and onion wedges. Place approximately 9 oysters on each skewer. Place in a large baking dish and dust with garlic powder. Broil, turning frequently until bacon and oysters are well-done.

Serves 6.

I don't know about you, but I'm nowhere near qualified to call myself a professional oyster shucker. These gents are more than qualified, billing themselves as oyster shuckers to the stars. In the celebrity department, I'd take Vernon Johnson over Brad Pitt any day.

Professional Oyster Shuckers

Since 1934

Bob Hastings
717-359-7794
Hanover, PA

Vernon Johnson
410-803-2578
Bel Air, MD

George Hastings
410-551-2636
Severn, MD

"Award-winning Shuckers to the Stars"

ROCKFISH AND OYSTERS BAKED IN PARCHMENT

 One way to royster (the old-fashioned word for making merry) with the oyster is to combine it with another Chesapeake favorite, the rockfish. This is an old Schmidt family recipe and, while it doesn't use crab, as per the tradition, it is oh, so good.

16   oysters in shells
3   tablespoons olive oil
1   carrot cut in 1-inch julienne strips
1   leek (white part), cut in 1-inch julienne strips

½   pound mushrooms, thinly sliced
¼   cup coarsely chopped fresh parsley
4   tablespoons fresh lemon juice
4   tablespoons dry white wine
    salt and freshly ground black pepper
4   tablespoons butter
8   ounces rockfish filets
4   pieces bakers' parchment or foil, approximately 12 by 14 inches
    olive oil for brushing on parchment

Shuck and drain the oysters and set aside.

Preheat oven to 475°F. In a heavy skillet, heat the olive oil. Add the carrots and sauté for 2 minutes. Add the leeks and mushrooms and cook until they begin to soften. Remove the pan from the heat, stir in the parsley, and let cool.

Fold each piece of parchment in half and cut into a lopsided oval (the shape of half a heart). Open the parchment hearts and spoon a fourth of the vegetable mixture on half of each piece. Top each with one fourth of the rockfish, 4 oysters, 1 tablespoon lemon juice, 1 tablespoon white wine, and salt and pepper to taste.

Seal the packages by folding the edges together, starting at one end and overlapping the folds. Place the packages on a baking sheet and lightly brush the tops and edges with olive oil. Bake for 10 to 12 minutes.

Serve warm, slicing the parchment open with a sharp knife and peeling it back. (I do this at the table.)

Serves 4.

*V*ernon *Johnson of Bel Air, Maryland, practices his art, shucking oysters. "Once you learn how to do it, the process becomes quite simple," Vernon says. One of his tricks: Don't jab the oyster knife right into the meat of the oyster; keep the blade against the shell to keep the oyster intact as you open it.*

Scalloped Oysters à la Raymond McAlwee

This lightly cheesy casserole should give you great insight into the everyday miracles that are possible when you combine oysters with cheese and parsley. Raymond, for one, believes fresh parsley is grievously under-used in most kitchens. "All too often, it's treated merely as a decorative garnish," he says, noting that parsley itself is an excellent ingredient to use when cooking—not just when you're preparing the plates. Amen, Raymond.

1	**pint oysters and liquor**
¼	**cup sliced celery**
¼	**cup minced onion**
2	**tablespoons butter**
1½	**cups buttery cracker crumbs**
½	**cup milk**
1	**tablespoon chopped fresh parsley**
1	**teaspoon lemon juice**
½	**teaspoon salt**
¼	**teaspoon garlic powder**
⅛	**teaspoon pepper**
½	**cup shredded cheddar cheese**
	additional chopped fresh parsley for garnish

Pour oysters and their liquor into a medium saucepan; simmer for 5 minutes or until the edges of the oysters begin to curl. Drain, reserving 2 tablespoons of the liquid; set aside.

Sauté the celery and onion in butter until tender; add cracker crumbs, milk, parsley, lemon juice, salt, garlic powder, and pepper. Mix well. Stir in the oysters and reserved liquor. Spoon the mixture into a buttered 1-quart casserole. Bake, uncovered, at 375°F for 15 minutes. Sprinkle cheese over the top and bake an additional 5 minutes or until the cheese melts. Garnish with chopped parsley.

Serves 4.

Two-time winner Scotty O'Lear presents his oysters to the crowd at the National Oyster Shucking Championship held in Leonardtown, Maryland. The shuckers are judged not only on how fast they can open oysters but also by how the oysters appear. Are they broken up? Full of shells? Then the score goes down. Luckily, Scotty doesn't have that problem too often.

OYSTER SHOOTERS

Photograph by Vince Lupo.

*R*eason to Smile: *King Oyster Dennis England, pictured here, was crowned at the 2000 National Oyster Cook-Off. The event drew some 20,000 people, who ate 50,000 oysters and drank 60 kegs of beer. That's about what we go through during a good weekend at the Crab Lab.*

If you like Guinness stout with your oysters, you're bound to enjoy this party favorite. Nothing nourishes the soul better. What do I recommend with oyster shooters? More oyster shooters—topped off by more Guinness.

SHOOTERS
- 1 cup Cocktail Sauce (recipe below)
- 1 cup Bloody Mary mix
- 1 pint oysters
  beer (Guinness stout)

Mix Cocktail Sauce and Bloody Mary mix together in a medium bowl. Place oysters in a shot glass with 2 tablespoons (1 ounce) of sauce. Serve with lemon wedges. Shoot as you would Schnapps. Follow each shooter with an ounce of beer.

Serves 6 with 4 shooters each.

COCKTAIL SAUCE
- 1 cup ketchup
- 1 tablespoon horseradish
- 1 teaspoon lemon juice
- 1 teaspoon Worcestershire sauce
- 1/4 teaspoon Tabasco sauce
  pinch of chili powder

Mix all ingredients together in a small bowl and refrigerate for 1 hour before serving.

Makes 1 cup.

OYSTERS IN CHAMPAGNE SAUCE

Oysters and champagne have always gone great together. Here, I combine them in this delightful dish. When matching champagne with oysters, most connoisseurs prefer a very dry champagne. Me, I drink whatever tastes good at the time.

⅔   **cup Hollandaise Sauce (see below)**
2   **shallots, finely chopped**
8   **tablespoons champagne**
16   **oysters on the half shell**

Make the Hollandaise Sauce. Add the shallots and champagne to the sauce. Spoon a little of the sauce on each oyster. Broil until bubbly (approximately 2 minutes) and serve.

Serves 4.

HOLLANDAISE SAUCE
2   **tablespoons water**
6   **peppercorns, slightly crushed**
1   **tablespoon white wine vinegar**
¾   **cup butter**
2   **egg yolks**
1   **tablespoon lemon juice**
     salt to taste

Place the water, crushed peppercorns, and vinegar in a small saucepan and reduce to about 1 tablespoon of liquid. Set aside.

Cut the butter into pieces and soften gently in a small saucepan. Remove from the heat. Beat the egg yolks, reduced liquid, and a little of the butter in a double boiler. When the mixture becomes creamy and slightly thick, add the remaining butter in a thin stream, beating briskly. Add lemon juice and salt to taste.

Remove sauce from heat as soon as it is thick. If the sauce starts to curdle, add a few drops of cold water and beat briskly for a few more minutes.

Makes 1 cup.

As past president of the Lexington Park Rotary Club, Adelle Pierce wears the crown and the cape of King Oyster at a recent oyster festival in Maryland. Long live the Oyster Queen—ahem—King.

107

GRACIE'S OYSTERS

You'll enjoy Gracie's oysters for break-fast, lunch or as a simple dinner. All you need is a nice salad or some creamy coleslaw and a glass of your favorite beer or wine.

24 oysters in shells
 6 slices bacon
    rock salt
 1 can (8 ounces) tomato sauce
 2 tablespoons lemon juice
 2 teaspoons sugar
 1 clove garlic, minced
½ teaspoon salt
½ teaspoon pepper
¼ teaspoon Tabasco sauce
 1 cup grated cheddar cheese

Shuck and drain the oysters and place each on the deep half of a shell. Partially cook bacon, drain, and cut each slice into 4 pieces.

Pour rock salt into a baking dish and place the oysters on top of it. In a small bowl, combine tomato sauce, lemon juice, sugar, garlic, salt, pepper, and Tabasco sauce, and mix well. Top each oyster with tomato sauce, a piece of bacon, and a sprinkle of cheese. Bake at 450°F for 10 minutes or until oyster edges curl and bacon is crisp.

Serves 6.

*R*eady, get set—shuck!

Photograph by Vince Lupo.

CARPETBAGGER STEAKS À LA DEAN GORE

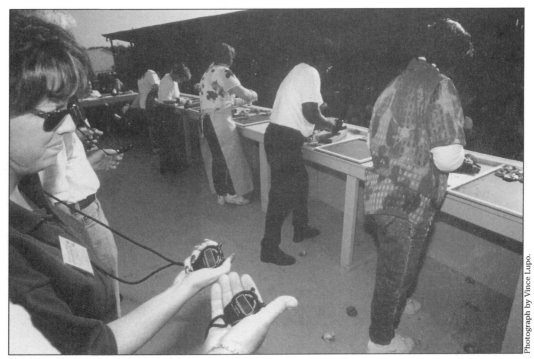

Here is my buddy Dean Gore's rendition of a classic oyster dish. In the traditional version, a thick steak with a pocket cut into it is used. The pocket is stuffed with seasoned fresh oysters and skewered shut before the steak is grilled.

1	**pint oysters and liquor**
1½	**cups soft white breadcrumbs**
½	**cup chopped onion**
¼	**cup chopped fresh parsley**
¼	**cup melted butter**
1	**tablespoon freshly squeeze lemon juice**
⅛	**teaspoon salt**
⅛	**teaspoon Tabasco sauce**
2	**tablespoons butter**
¼	**cup water**
6	**cube steaks**
	salt and pepper

Drain oysters, reserving the liquor. Combine oysters, liquor, breadcrumbs, onion, and parsley. Combine butter, lemon juice, salt, and Tabasco sauce and add to the oyster mixture; mix thoroughly.

Place about ¼ cup oyster stuffing on each steak. Wrap steaks around stuffing and secure with wooden picks. In a skillet, brown rolled-up steaks on all sides in 2 tablespoons of butter for about 10 minutes. Lower the heat and cook, covered, for 5 minutes.

Remove the steaks to a warm platter. To make pan gravy, add water to the pan and heat, stirring and scraping the bottom of the pan. Serve over steaks.

Serves 6.

No easy job: Timekeepers at the National Oyster Shucking Championships can't drop their guard for a second. As soon as their shuckers give the signal that they've completed the tray, the clocks stop. Then the slurping begins.

Photograph by Vince Lupo.

OYSTER COCKTAIL FOR A CROWD

If shell oysters are not available, purchase 2 gallons of shucked oysters and serve in lettuce cups.

600 oysters in shells
  2 quarts ketchup
  1 pint lemon juice
  1 quart celery, finely chopped
  1 cup horseradish, grated
  2 tablespoons salt
  1 tablespoon Tabasco sauce
     crushed ice

Shuck oysters, reserving the deep shells and discarding the liquor. For each serving, cover a plate with crushed ice. Arrange 6 shells on the ice and place an oyster in each. Make a sauce by mixing the ketchup, lemon juice, celery, horseradish, salt, and Tabasco sauce. Place a small dish of sauce in the middle of each plate.
Serves 100.

The very first oyster ever eaten— at first fright, then delight. This drawing by Sol Eytinge first appeared in Harper's Weekly *on October 4, 1879.*

110

Tom Vernon's Oyster Salad

Tom Vernon, who wouldn't dare eat any meat product, will eat any seafood put in front of him. This is one of his favorite recipes—of course it's a healthy one! Not to mention delicious.

1	**pint oysters and liquor**
1	**cup olive oil**
4	**tablespoons fresh lemon juice**
½	**cup chopped green pepper**
½	**cup chopped red pepper**
½	**cup chopped yellow pepper**
3	**scallions, finely chopped**
2	**garlic cloves, minced**
1	**tablespoon Dijon mustard**
2	**tablespoons chopped fresh parsley**
2	**teaspoons chopped fresh dill**
2	**teaspoons crumbled dried rosemary**
	salt and freshly ground black pepper
	radicchio and endive leaves

In a small saucepan, combine the oysters and liquor. Cook over medium-low heat just until the edges curl, about 2 minutes.

In a bowl, whisk together the oil, lemon juice, peppers, scallions, garlic, mustard, parsley, dill, rosemary, and salt and pepper to taste. Stir in the oysters. Cover and refrigerate for 4 hours or overnight.

Arrange the radicchio and endive on serving plates. Top with the oyster salad.

Serves 6.

For those of us who love our oysters and can't get our fill, the St. Mary's County Oyster Festival is a wonderful place to, well, get our fill.

Photograph by Vince Lupo.

111

TIMMY'S OYSTER SHOOTERS

Photograph by Vince Lupo.

 *The night before you plan to serve these delicious oyster shooters, there is one thing you must do: Put the vodka in the freezer to chill overnight. And remember what the Bible says: "Drink no longer water, but use an oyster shooter for thy stomach's sake." —* TIMOTHY 5:23.

> 1   **pint oysters**
> 24   **ounces vodka (1 ounce per shooter)**
>   **cocktail sauce**
>   **horseradish**
>   **Tabasco sauce**

For each shooter, put a raw oyster, 1 ounce of vodka, a pinch of horseradish, a dab of cocktail sauce, and a dash of Tabasco sauce in a shot glass.

Serves 24.

*N*ow *revitalized, the Fells Point neighborhood of Baltimore was once constantly humming with commercial boats of all kinds, powered by sail and steam. During the day, steamers crowded the piers, and in the afternoon, they headed back to the Bay for the return home. Likewise, skipjacks, clippers, and other ships of sail frequented Fells Point at various times in its history. This legacy is celebrated today with the annual Fells Point Festival, where you'll find plenty of 18th-century history and lots of foam crab hats to boot.*

OYSTER CACCIATORE DONALD HAMMETT

Cacciatore, the American-Italian term, refers to food prepared "hunter style," with tomatoes, onions, various herbs and sometimes wine. Chicken cacciatore is the most popular such dish, of course. But that will change as people turn on to the oysterized version.

2	medium onions, thinly sliced
1	quart oysters
2	cloves garlic, minced
1	can (16 ounces) tomatoes
1	can (8 ounces) tomato sauce
1	teaspoon salt
¼	teaspoon pepper
2	crushed oregano leaves
½	teaspoon dried basil, crushed
½	teaspoon celery seed
1	bay leaf
¼	cup dry white wine

Place sliced onions in the bottom of a crockpot. Add oysters and the rest of the ingredients. Cover and cook on low for 6 to 8 hours or on high for 3 to 4 hours. Serve over buttered saltine crackers.

Serves 6.

*B*ack in the 1980s, the Maryland Watermen's Association held an annual Chesapeake Appreciation Days event. The oyster-cooking contest was a major draw along with the skipjack races. The festival's popularity diminished each year, though, as it always seemed to be cold and rainy. Today, alas, we can only appreciate that fine event in our memories. (Some oyster trivia: Donald Hammett won the contest in 1980.)

URBANNA CREEK CELERIED OYSTERS

One of my favorite ways to entertain is with oyster-themed dinners. I try to put out a number of various oyster dishes, some traditional, some a little unusual—like this delicious dish. It's always a good idea to serve something along with the oysters, too. I like potato dishes—say, mashed, with garlic—and, of course, some good chilled wine.

1	**tablespoon butter**
1	**pint oysters and liquor**
2	**tablespoons chopped celery hearts and leaves**
	salt
	cayenne pepper
½	**cup sherry**
4	**buttered toast points**

In a saucepan, melt the butter, add the oysters and liquor, and stir in the chopped celery. Season with salt and cayenne pepper to taste. Let the mixture cook for 5 minutes, until the edges of the oysters curl. Add the sherry and bring the mixture up to heat. Pour over toast points and serve hot.

Serves 4.

31st annual
URBANNA OYSTER FESTIVAL
FRIDAY & SATURDAY, NOVEMBER 4 & 5, 1988
OFFICIAL PROGRAM

The 1988 winner of the Urbanna Oyster Festival print competition was Richmond, Virginia, artist Dale Totty. The painting shows two oystermen working their shaft tongs as they watch a flock of geese flying high overhead.

URBANNA BAKED OYSTERS

This wonderful recipe comes from the Northern Neck of Virginia, a uniquely Chesapeake-flavored area surrounded by natural waterways and laced with creeks and inlets. The oysters grown here are of breathtaking beauty, as are the local mushrooms.

2   cups packed sourdough bread cubes
1   cup coarsely chopped mushrooms
¼   cup freshly grated Parmigiano-Reggiano cheese
¼   cup chopped fresh parsley
3   tablespoons butter, cut in small pieces
1   tablespoon lemon juice
½   teaspoon dried thyme
½   teaspoon dried basil
½   teaspoon salt
½   teaspoon Tabasco sauce
½   teaspoon freshly ground black pepper
24   oysters in shells

Place the bread cubes and mushrooms in a food processor and pulse to combine. Add the Parmigiano-Reggiano cheese, parsley, butter, lemon juice, thyme, basil, salt, Tabasco sauce, and black pepper. Process until the particles are well chopped and pea-like in texture, about 30 seconds. Set aside.

Shuck the oysters and place them in the deep halves of the shells. Cover each oyster loosely with 1 rounded tablespoon of the bread-crumb-mushroom mixture, coating the entire surface of the oyster. Arrange the oysters on a baking sheet and place on the middle shelf of the oven. Bake at 475°F until the topping is golden, 6 to 8 minutes. Serve immediately.

Serves 4.

ROYSTER WITH THE OYSTER

"Let us royster with the oyster—in the shorter days and moister,

That are brought by brown September, with its roguish final R;

For breakfast or for supper, on the under shell or upper,

Of dishes he's the daisy, and of shell-fish he's the star.

We try him as they fry him, and even as they pie him;

We're partial to him luscious in a roast;

We boil and broil him, we vinegar-and-oil him,

And O he is delicious stewed with toast.

We eat him with tomatoes, and the salad with potatoes,

Nor look him o'er with horror when he follows the coleslaw;

And neither does he fret us if he marches after lettuce,

And abreast of cayenne pepper when his majesty is raw.

So welcome with September to the knife and glowing ember,

Juicy darling of our dainties, dispossessor of the clam!

To the oyster, then a hoister, with him a royal royster,

We shall whoop it through the land of heathen jam."

—*THE DETROIT FREE PRESS*, OCTOBER 12, 1889

SCALLOPED CORN AND OYSTERS

People who love oysters also tend to like corn. The two have a tasty affinity for one another, as you'll find in this dish. Pop Schmidt made this one many times, and it wasn't until I left home as a young man that I started missing it. Scalloped corn and oysters is, for me, the greatest comfort food.

1	stick butter
2	cups crushed saltine crackers
1	can (15–16 ounces) cream-style corn
½	cup half-and-half
½	teaspoon salt
¼	teaspoon pepper
1	pint oysters
2 or 3	shakes Tabasco sauce

Melt the butter in a large saucepan. Stir the crushed crackers into the butter. Mix together the corn, half-and-half, salt, pepper, and Tabasco sauce. In a greased 8-by-8-inch casserole, layer the ingredients in this order: half of the oysters, half of the cracker mixture, all of the corn mixture, then the rest of the oysters and the rest of the cracker mixture. Bake at 350°F for 20 minutes or until hot and bubbly.

Serves 6.

17TH ANNUAL J. MILLARD TAWES OYSTER & BULL ROAST

Saturday, October 20, 2001

1 - 5 p.m. (Rain or Shine)

Somers Cove Marina Pavilion

Crisfield, Maryland

All you can eat!

$25.00 single

Table for 8 - $160.00

Sponsored by Crisfield Heritage Foundation

"Blessed if I don't think that ven a man's wery poor, he rushes out of his lodgings, and eats oysters in reg'lar desperation."

—CHARLES DICKENS
IN *THE PICKWICK PAPERS*

DOWN THE HATCH OYSTER SHOOTERS

 Up to the lips and over the gums, look out stomach, here she comes!

6   **vodka glasses, chilled**
6   **oysters in shells**
     Tabasco sauce
1   **tablespoon minced shallots**
1   **tablespoon finely minced lemon grass, white part only**
6   **ounces Absolut Citron vodka, chilled**

Shuck the oysters, discarding liquor and shells. In each vodka glass, place an oyster, Tabasco sauce to taste, and some shallots and lemon grass. Top each glass off with an ounce of vodka.

Serves 6.

"The Oyster Eaters" by L. Bouilly, published in 1825, highlights this flyer for the Annapolis Seafood Market, "where select oysters are kept for sale." Great, now let's eat them.

117

STEWED TO THE GILLS OYSTERS

There's more than one way to stew an oyster, as witnessed by this unusual dish. While the Southern Comfort might leave your head spinning, your heart will wind up winning— and it'll get warm in the process.

1	quart oysters and liquor
12	slices bacon, cut in half
1	teaspoon salt
½	teaspoon freshly ground black pepper
	splash of Tabasco sauce
2	teaspoons tomato paste
1	cup Southern Comfort
8	slices toast, each cut in half

Drain the oysters and discard liquor. Broil the bacon until almost done but still limp. Drain well and wrap each oyster in a piece of bacon, tucking the ends under. Place the bacon-wrapped oysters under the broiler until the bacon is done cooking.

Combine the salt, pepper, Tabasco sauce, tomato paste, and Southern Comfort in the top of a double boiler over warm water. Place two toast halves on each of 8 small, warmed plates and then three oysters on top of the toast. Pour the sauce over all.

Serves 8.

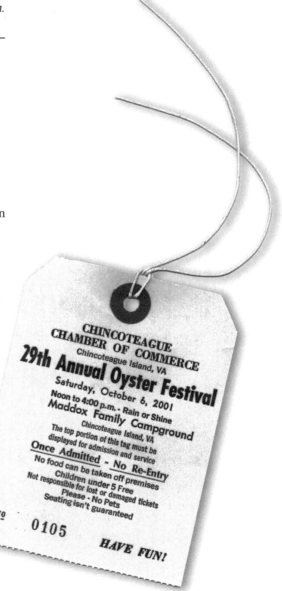

*V*isitors to this magical festival are in for a special treat. The menu offers steamed crabs, steamed oysters, oysters on the half-shell, oyster stew, oyster fritters, and fried oysters—along with a few trimmings like coleslaw, potato salad and hush puppies. All right, you get the car warmed up and I'll get my oyster knife. We're going to Chincoteague!

TORCH BEARERS

This recipe comes from the hardpan world of professional oystermen, who, being purists, prefer their oysters uncooked and unadorned. In addition to the rum, I like to add a dash of lemon and Tabasco sauce and down the just-extinguished bivalves with a frosty beer. This is one of our favorite pastimes when hanging around the Crab Lab kitchen—largely, but not solely, because it involves fire. Must be a cave-man thing.

> 6 oysters in shells
> ½ pint 151-proof dark rum
>   black pepper
>   Tabasco sauce

Shuck the oysters and place them in a metal pie plate. Pour the rum over the oysters. Set them afire and flavor these blue-blazing oysters with black pepper and Tabasco sauce.
Serves 6.

When the fire is out, munch slowly with a certain quiet dignity and ceremony which will accentuate the rum taste and aroma.

—FROM *CHESAPEAKE FACT, FICTION, FUN*
BY FAY AND FRED TILP, 1988, HERITAGE BOOKS, INC.

Scott and Paige Yoder of Hummelstown, Pennsylvania, took advantage of the 2002 Chincoteague Oyster Festival to tie the knot. You can tell from the sign overhead that they've apparently gotten a little lost on their way to the "married fried oysters" stand.

119

SCALDED OYSTERS

There are not many recipes as easy as this one. And there are not many as good tasting. I want you to try'em tonight!

24   **oysters in shells**
2   **sticks butter**
½   **teaspoon seafood seasoning**
    Tabasco sauce
    lemons

Scrub the oyster shells with a wire brush under cold running water. Fill a large kettle with water and bring it to a boil. Lower the oysters into the boiling water in a wire basket and return the water to a boil. Cook until the shells open. Remove the oysters from the water and allow them to cool until you can touch the shells. Remove and discard the flat shell and serve the oysters on the deep shell.

Melt the butter and mix in the seafood seasoning. Serve the oysters with the seasoned butter, Tabasco sauce, and freshly cut lemons.

Serves 4.

What do you do after slurping a couple of dozen oysters? My strategy: Rest up, flutter your eyes for about five minutes, and go back for more.

CHAPTER 6
Nostalgia On the Half-Shell
(The Joy of Oysters)

Illustration by B. West Clinedinst, *Harper's Weekly*, March 2, 1889.

OYSTERS IN BROWN SAUCE

Harper's Weekly, March 16, 1872.

This illustration by B. West Clinedinst gives a wonderful snapshot of Maryland's oyster business as it was in the 1880s. Here, an oyster speculator tests some cargo. Now that's one of the few jobs I've ever found attractive.

All the recipes in this chapter are served in the oysters' shells (Neptune's china, I call them). When you shuck the oysters, be sure to reserve the deeper of the two shells for serving. Also, place the serving shells on a bed of rock salt. That keeps them in position and also helps the oysters to stay hot. Happiness on the half-shell!

36	oysters in shells
3	tablespoons butter
3	teaspoons all-purpose flour
	salt and pepper
¾	cup heavy cream

Shuck and drain the oysters, reserving the liquor. Dry the oysters between towels and pan broil them until the edges curl; set aside.

In a saucepan, melt the butter and allow it to brown. Add the flour and salt and pepper to taste. Pour the cream in slowly and then add ¼ cup of the reserved oyster liquor. Cook, stirring constantly, until thickened. Spoon this brown sauce over the oysters, place under the broiler to bring up to heat, and serve.

Serves 6.

HOT OYSTER CANAPES
(page 28)

Color insert photographs by award-winning photographer Vince Lupo.

NANTICOKE OYSTER FRITTERS
(page 57)

LORD'S GIFT OYSTER PYE
(page 95)

ROCKFISH AND OYSTERS BAKED IN PARCHMENT
(page 104)

CAESAR SALAD WITH CORNMEAL FRIED OYSTERS
(page 126)

OYSTERS ON THE HALF-SHELL (WITH A TRIO OF SAUCES)
(page 135)

OYSTERS BENEDICT PIER
(page 138)

TOLLY POINT ROAD OYSTERS ROCKEFELLER
(page 172)

WARE RIVER BROILED OYSTERS

Sprinkled with spirited cayenne and brought to their knees by plenty of fresh lemon, these oysters should be popped whole into the mouth so you can savor the perfect blending of delicious juices and bubbly melted cheese.

24	oysters in shells
1	lemon
	dash of cayenne pepper
1	stick butter
¼	cup flour
1	cup dry white wine
½	cup heavy cream
¼	teaspoon salt
	freshly ground black pepper
1	tablespoon minced fresh thyme
½	cup grated Parmigiano-Reggiano cheese

Shuck the oysters, discarding the oyster liquor and reserving the deep bottom shells. Wash and dry the shells and place each oyster in a shell. Squeeze lemon juice over them and sprinkle with cayenne pepper.

Make a roux with the butter and flour. When smooth, blend in the wine, cream, salt, pepper and thyme. Bring this sauce just to a boil, then spoon over the oysters. Sprinkle each oyster with a little Parmigiano-Reggiano cheese. Broil for for 4 to 5 minutes.

Serves 4.

I purchased this postcard at an antiques shop on Maryland's Eastern Shore. The card was sent from Border's Oysters in Baltimore on February 12, 1895. It arrived at Mr. Ottoway's house in Westfield, New York, on February 14, 1895. Not bad!

123

DUKE OF GLOUCESTER OYSTERS

If first impressions are lasting ones, you'll never forget these savory delights accented with bacon, basil, and cheese and topped with some crunchy celery.

12   **oysters in shells**
      rock salt
2   **slices provolone cheese**
2   **slices bacon**
12   **fresh opal basil leaves, chopped**
6   **tablespoons finely chopped celery**

Shuck the oysters, discarding the oyster liquor and reserving the deep bottom shells. Wash and dry the shells, place each oyster in a shell, and place the shells on a bed of rock salt in a shallow pan.

Cut the cheese and bacon into 12 pieces. Top each oyster with basil, then celery, then cheese, then bacon. Broil until the bacon is cooked.

Serves 2.

Harper's Weekly, March 16, 1872.

The waters from which oysters are harvested are frequently inspected and analyzed, as are the oysters themselves. Today, oyster packers operate under a microscope of regulations and rules, and every jar of oysters is labeled with the salient details of how, when, and where the bivalves were harvested and packed. In this old Harper's *illustration, we see a man at work soldering the tops onto cans of oysters.*

MO'S GRILLED BARBECUED OYSTERS

Barbecuing oysters in their shells is one of the more pleasant—and elemental—ways to prepare them. By adding a few sticks of hickory wood to your fire, you can get a little smoky flavor into the oysters, the perfect accompaniment to my buddy Mo's special barbecue sauce.

⅓   **cup Tabasco sauce**
¼   **cup Worcestershire sauce**
2   **tablespoons fresh lemon juice**
1   **tablespoon extra-virgin olive oil**
¼   **teaspoon salt**
¼   **teaspoons cracked black pepper**
4   **cloves garlic, minced**
48   **oysters in shells**
¼   **cup chopped fresh flat-leaf parsley**

8   **lemon wedges**
    crushed dried red pepper flakes

Prepare the grill. Make barbecue sauce by combining Tabasco sauce, Worcestershire sauce, lemon juice, olive oil, salt, black pepper, and garlic in a saucepan.

Place the saucepan and oysters on the grill rack. Grill for 5 minutes or until oysters begin to open. Remove oysters from heat and open them with an oyster knife. Leave the oysters on their half-shells.

Sprinkle the oysters with parsley and crushed red pepper flakes and drizzle with barbecue sauce. Serve with lemon wedges.

Serves 8.

This vintage Harper's Weekly *illustration shows an oyster house worker preparing containers of oysters for the market. I'll take a bushel!*

CAESAR SALAD WITH CORNMEAL FRIED OYSTERS

Tijuana takes credit for this salad, said to have been concocted one evening from the only ingredients left in the kitchen. My question is, who left the oysters?

OYSTERS

	vegetable oil for deep frying
1	cup cornmeal
½	teaspoon salt
½	teaspoon freshly ground black pepper
½	teaspoon cayenne pepper
16	oysters in shells

SALAD

6	anchovy fillets, soaked in 4 tablespoons milk
1	clove garlic, left whole
½	cup olive oil
1	egg, cooked in shell for 1 minute
1	head romaine lettuce
	juice of 1 small lemon
	salt and pepper
4	tablespoons grated Parmigiano-Reggiano cheese

Oysters: Heat the vegetable oil to 350°F. In a large bowl, season the cornmeal with the salt, black pepper, and cayenne pepper. Shuck the oysters, discarding the shells and liquor. Dip each oysters in the cornmeal mixture and fry until golden brown, about 2 minutes. Transfer to absorbent paper to drain.

Ck for 156 Leave the anchovies to soak in the milk for 15 minutes, then rinse them and pat them dry on paper towels. Chop them roughly.

Crush the garlic and leave it in the olive oil for about 30 minutes. Break the cooked egg into a bowl and beat well with the lemon juice and salt and pepper to taste. Tear the lettuce into bite-size pieces and toss with the oil and anchovies. Add the egg mixture and toss to coat well. Place in a serving bowl and place the oysters on top. Sprinkle with cheese. Serve at room temperature.

Serves 4.

Illustration by John Dalziel.

"Mine Oysters: Dredging Boats in the Chesapeake," a vintage John Dalziel illustration from Harper's Weekly, *1872.*

126

STOCKTON OYSTER BAKE

Requiring very little effort to prepare, this tantalizing oyster and scallop bake should create a stir with your guests. While I don't put lemon juice in my Hollandaise sauce, you can add a tablespoon or so—or simply provide fresh lemon wedges and let each diner decide.

OYSTERS
4	slices bacon, diced
16	white mushrooms, sliced
1	cup bay scallops, sliced
1/2	cup all-purpose flour
16	oysters in shells
	vegetable oil for frying
1	bunch fresh spinach, trimmed and rinsed well

HOLLANDAISE SAUCE
1	cup butter
3	egg yolks, lightly beaten
	splash of water
	dash of Tabasco sauce
	salt

Oysters: In a large frying pan, sauté diced bacon, mushrooms, and scallops for about 5 minutes. Shuck the oysters, discarding the oyster liquor and reserving the deep bottom shells.

Lightly flour the oysters. In a second frying pan, brown them on both sides, adding vegetable oil as needed. Cover them with the spinach and place a lid on the pan. Cook just until the spinach is wilted. Divide the spinach into 16 parts and place some spinach and an oyster in each shell. Top with mushroom, scallop, and bacon mixture. Cover with Hollandaise sauce.

Hollandaise Sauce: Melt the butter in a small saucepan. In a bowl, whisk the melted butter into the egg yolks, water, Tabasco, and salt to taste.

Serves 4.

Here's a wonderful old illustration from Frank Leslie's Illustrated Newspaper, *done by a staff artist and published July 11, 1885. It's titled "Shuckers at Work." Notice the shells piling up at their feet, presumably from a single day's work.*

OCEAN VIEW STUFFED OYSTERS

To be a nice guy, I told a surprise visitor that this recipe was for two. But I could've eaten the whole dozen, if only she would've let me.

1   **cup dried breadcrumbs**
½   **cup finely chopped fresh parsley**
½   **cup grated Parmigiano-Reggiano cheese**
1   **teaspoon chopped fresh basil**
1   **teaspoon chopped fresh oregano**
3   **tablespoons olive oil**
12   **oysters in shells**

Mix breadcrumbs, parsley, Parmigiano-Reggiano cheese, basil, oregano, and olive oil. Add more oil if necessary to moisten throughout.

Shuck the oysters, discarding the oyster liquor and reserving the deep bottom shells. Put each oyster in a shell and sprinkle on a generous amount of breadcrumb topping. Broil 3 to 5 minutes, or until topping is golden brown. Serve immediately.

Serves 2.

This Harper's Weekly *illustration ran on March 16, 1872 and is believed to be the work of famed Harper's artist Johnson-Dyer.*

SMITH ISLAND OYSTERS ON THE HALF-SHELL

Oysters and bacon just go together. Sometimes I shuck a few and simply put a piece of bacon atop each one and broil them in their half-shells. Point them up with a dash of lemon and a little Tabasco sauce and you'll be in heaven. This recipe also takes advantage of some other classic oyster accompaniments: butter, breadcrumbs and horseradish.

48	oysters in shells
	rock salt
1	teaspoon Tabasco sauce
2	tablespoons Worcestershire sauce
2	tablespoons ketchup
2	tablespoons horseradish
2	tablespoons vinegar
4	tablespoons lemon juice
4	green onions, minced (tops and all)
8	slices bacon
	breadcrumbs
1	stick butter

Shuck the oysters, discarding the oyster liquor and reserving the deep bottom shells. Put an oyster in each shell.

Line the bottom of each pie pan with rock salt. Arrange 6 to 8 oyster shells in each pie pan. Mix the Tabasco sauce, Worcestershire sauce, ketchup, horseradish, vinegar, lemon juice, and green onions, and put 1½ tablespoons of this sauce on top of each oyster in the shell.

Cut bacon to match the lengths of the shells and lay a piece of bacon on top of each oyster. Cover each with breadcrumbs and ½ teaspoon butter. Broil 5 to 7 minutes. Serve in the pie pan (put each pie pan on top of a regular plate). The salt keeps the oysters hot.

Serves 6 to 8.

This March 16, 1872 Harper's Weekly *illustration shows some hardworking folks packing oysters. We can only hope they managed to pop one into their mouths now and then.*

129

EDINBURGH OYSTERS ON THE HALF-SHELL

Vinegar, which literally means "sour wine," can be made from other things, such as cider, grain alcohol, malt, and rice. Vinegar can be flavored with herbs or fruit, too. Maybe you can tell that I'm a big vinegar fan. It certainly adds a nice kick to this dish.

8   **shallots, peeled and minced**
1   **cup red wine vinegar**
36 **oysters in shells**

Shuck the oysters, discarding the oyster liquor and reserving the deep bottom shells. Place an oyster in each shell. In a blender, purée the shallots with the vinegar until smooth. Spoon about 1 teaspoon of this sauce over each oyster to cover with a thin layer. Serve immediately.

Serves 6.

This Harper's Weekly illustration is titled "Mine-Oysters—Filling with Liquor." I wonder if the health department would allow today's oyster house workers to smoke pipes. Doubtful.

BALTIMORE BROILED OYSTERS

This is an old Charm City recipe that uses soft breadcrumbs to help bind the onion, celery, and bell pepper. It then uses dry breadcrumbs for crunch. I guarantee you'll munch a bunch. Just a hunch. Maybe for lunch? Uhm, yeah.

24	oysters in shells
4	tablespoons butter
1	cup chopped onion
½	cup chopped celery
½	bell pepper, chopped
1	cup soft breadcrumbs
¼	teaspoon salt
	dash of Tabasco sauce
2	egg yolks
2	teaspoons chopped fresh parsley
1	cup dry breadcrumbs
	Parmigiano-Reggiano cheese

Shuck the oysters, reserving the oyster liquor and the deep bottom shells. Place the bottom shells in baking pans.

In a saucepan, melt the butter and sauté the onion, celery, and bell pepper until golden. Add the oysters, 1 cup of the oyster liquor, the soft breadcrumbs, salt, and Tabasco sauce. Simmer for 15 minutes and set aside.

In a small bowl, beat the egg yolks and combine them with the parsley. Stir this mixture into the oyster mixture and divide among the oyster shells. Top with dry breadcrumbs and Parmigiano-Reggiano cheese and bake at 375°F for 25 minutes.

Serves 4.

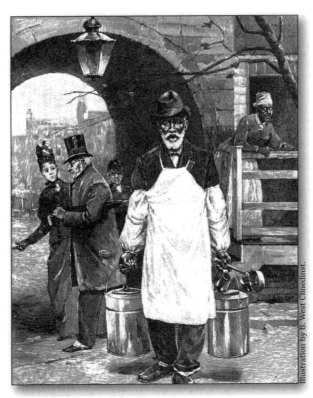

This illustration from the March 2, 1889 edition of Harper's Weekly *shows a Southern oyster peddler preparing to take his wares to market.*

131

PIPER'S PESTO OYSTERS

My pal Pat Piper proudly presents his pesto oysters, which I often serve for Sunday brunch. This has to be one of the best oyster recipes I've ever tried. You'll be surprised at how naturally the zing of pesto goes with the rich, briny oyster undertones.

12	**oysters in shells**
½	**cup pesto sauce**
4	**tablespoons breadcrumbs**
4	**tablespoons grated Parmigiano-Reggiano cheese**
12	**pieces pimiento for garnish**

Shuck the oysters, reserving the deep shells and discarding the liquor and top shells. Place the oysters, in their shells, on a baking sheet. Top each oyster with a sprinkling of breadcrumbs, a small amount of pesto sauce, some Parmigiano-Reggiano cheese, and a piece of pimiento. Put under the broiler for 5 to 7 minutes or until the oysters have curled.

Serves 2.

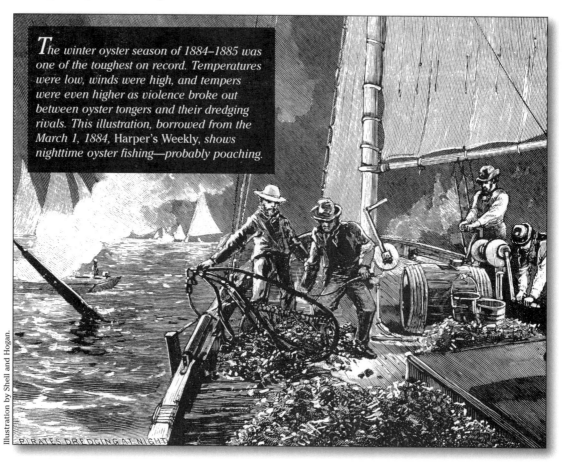

The winter oyster season of 1884–1885 was one of the toughest on record. Temperatures were low, winds were high, and tempers were even higher as violence broke out between oyster tongers and their dredging rivals. This illustration, borrowed from the March 1, 1884, Harper's Weekly, *shows nighttime oyster fishing—probably poaching.*

Illustration by Shell and Hogan.

PIRATES DREDGING AT NIGHT

HEYSER BAKED OYSTERS

Here is an uncomplicated yet delicious oyster dish. Sometimes, keeping it simple is the way to go. In this case, tasting is believing.

1	**egg**
1	**tablespoon ice water**
36	**oysters in shells**
	fine dry breadcrumbs
	butter
	rock salt

Shuck the oysters, reserving the deep shells and discarding the liquor and top shells.

Beat the egg and water together. Dip each oyster in this mixture, roll in breadcrumbs, and arrange them in their shells. Dot them generously with butter. Arrange the shells on a bed of rock salt and bake at 450°F until golden brown, about 5 minutes.

Serves 6.

This illustration depicts Maryland police steamers chasing a pirate fleet. The Maryland Oyster Navy, chartered by the Maryland General Assembly, used worn-out Civil War tugs. And from the looks of this drawing, they had their hands full.

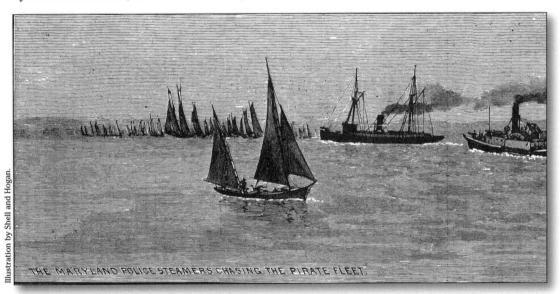

THE MARYLAND POLICE STEAMERS CHASING THE PIRATE FLEET.

Illustration by Shell and Hogan.

OYSTERS CHATEAU VIN-MER

 You may use additional seasonings for this recipe, but I wouldn't go overboard. You don't want to mask the oysters' true flavor.

36 oysters in shells
    rock salt
½   teaspoon cayenne pepper
½   teaspoon garlic powder
1   teaspoon onion powder
½   teaspoon finely crushed dried parsley
    salt

9   teaspoons fresh lemon juice
    (¼ teaspoon for each oyster)
4½ teaspoons olive oil (⅛ teaspoon for
    each oyster)
9   teaspoons finely chopped green onions
    (¼ teaspoon for each oysters)
    crackers

Shuck the oysters, reserving the deep shells and discarding the liquor and top shells. Place the shells on half an inch of rock salt in shallow baking pans, and place an oyster in each shell.

Mix the cayenne pepper, garlic powder, onion powder, and parsley in a small mixing bowl. Add salt if needed. Sprinkle the oysters with these mixed seasonings and top each with lemon juice, olive oil, and teaspoon green onions. Bake at 400°F for 10 to 15 minutes, just until the edges of the oysters begin to curl. Serve with crackers.

Serves 6.

Illustration by Frank Adams.

A Maryland state police steamer overtakes an oyster pirate on the Chesapeake Bay in this January 7, 1888, illustration from Frank Leslie's Illustrated Newspaper. *I'm not sure whom I'm rooting for here! I've always had a soft spot for piratical types.*

OYSTERS ON THE HALF-SHELL WITH A TRIO OF SAUCES

When I serve up this trio of sauces, I set the oysters on a platter spread with crushed ice and pass the sauces separately so guests can sample all three.

OYSTERS

36   oysters in shells
 7   cups crushed ice
 1   lemon
     freshly cracked black pepper
     wine vinegar

COCKTAIL SAUCE

 1   cup chili sauce
 2   tablespoons prepared horseradish
 2   tablespoons lemon juice
 2   tablespoons finely chopped celery

SOUR CREAM DILL SAUCE

 ½   cup sour cream
 ½   cup mayonnaise
 1   tablespoon chopped fresh dill weed
 ¼   cup finely chopped dill pickle
 1   teaspoon finely chopped parsley

RÉMOULADE SAUCE

1½   cups mayonnaise
 2   tablespoons Dijon mustard
 1   teaspoon anchovy paste
 ¼   cup chopped cornichons (gherkin
     pickles)
 1   tablespoon capers
 ¼   cup minced fresh parsley
 ¼   cup minced fresh chervil

Oysters: Scrub oyster shells under running cold water. Shuck them just before serving, discard the top shells, and strain and reserve the liquor. Arrange the oysters in the deep shells on a bed of ice and pour the liquor over them. Serve with a wedge of lemon, a bit of cracked pepper, a splash of vinegar, or one of the three savory sauces.

Sauces: Mix ingredients for each sauce in a small serving bowl.

Serves 6.

Sketch by Walter Somers.

In this illustration, oyster navy sloop Nannie Merryman *exchanges fire with dredging schooner* Eugene. Eugene *had rammed and capsized tonging boats but was fast enough to evade arrest.*

135

CEDAR POINT OYSTER BAKE

Peeled, grated fresh ginger greatly enhances the taste of many sauces. It can also be chopped and put through a garlic press, bringing a wonderful, gingery juice to this recipe.

12 **oysters in shells**
     rock salt
  4 **tablespoons butter**
  1 **tablespoon minced fresh ginger**
  1 **rib celery cut into 2-inch matchstick**
     strips
  2 **carrots cut into 2-inch matchstick strips**
¼ **teaspoon salt**
     freshly ground black pepper

Shuck the oysters, reserving the deep shells and discarding the liquor and top shells. Place the oysters on half an inch of rock salt in a shallow pan.

In a skillet over medium heat, melt the butter. Add the ginger and sauté for 1 minute. Add the celery and carrots and sauté for 4 to 5 minutes, or until vegetables are tender. Stir in the salt and pepper to taste.

Spoon some of the vegetables over each oyster. Bake at 400°F for 8 to 10 minutes, or until the oysters are plump and heated through.

Serves 2.

THE PIRATES ATTACKING THE POLICE SCHOONER "JULIA HAMILTON"

This illustration depicts oyster pirates attacking the Maryland police boat Julia Hamilton. *A bitter gun battle ensued. Tussles like these would often last for hours, until one side ran out of ammo, having fired off thousands of rounds. Every time the dredgers won, they blew horns and shouted out Indian war cries. Sounds like a late night at the Crab Lab.*

OYSTERS WITH COMPOUND BUTTER

 Did you know that it takes the cream from 18 pints of milk to make a pound of butter? I didn't until I created this recipe.

1   **stick butter**
1   **teaspoon chopped fresh tarragon**
1   **teaspoon chopped fresh parsley**
1   **teaspoon chopped fresh garlic**
1   **teaspoon fresh lemon juice**
24 **oysters in shells**
    salt and pepper

Cut the butter into fingernail-size pieces and place in a bowl. Beat with a wooden spoon until soft and fluffy. Add the herbs and garlic and beat in the lemon juice a few drops at a time. Add salt and pepper to taste.

Spread the butter in a strip about 5 inches long and 1½ inches wide on a sheet of waxed paper. Roll the butter back and forth inside the roll of paper until it feels smooth and even. Twist the ends of the paper and chill.

Shuck the oysters, leaving the meat on the deep shells and discarding the top shells and liquor. Place the shells on a baking sheet.

Cut off slices of the butter, place them on the oysters, and broil until the butter melts and the oysters curl.

Serves 2.

This illustration depicts pirates dredging at night.
HARPER'S WEEKLY,
MARCH 1, 1884

137

OYSTERS BENEDICT PIER

Shallots are formed more like garlic than onions, with a head composed of multiple cloves. They're plump and (when fresh) firm and are valued for their mild onion flavor. You can, in fact, use them as substitutes for onions. I like them because they're usually a little sweeter than onions, and more subtle in flavor.

16	oysters in shells
8	slices Canadian bacon
4	English muffins
2	tablespoons butter
1	tablespoon dry sherry
2	tablespoons finely chopped shallots
	freshly ground white pepper
1½	cups warm Hollandaise sauce
	(see recipe on page 127)

Shuck and drain oysters, discarding shells and reserving ¼ cup of the liquor.

In a skillet, lightly sauté the Canadian bacon in butter. Split the English muffins and toast them in the broiler. In a saucepan, heat the butter, oyster liquor, and sherry and simmer the shallots until tender; add the oysters, season with pepper, and cook until the oysters are hot and plump.

Place two muffin halves on each plate, and distribute the bacon, oysters, and some of the pan juices among the muffins. Ladle on a generous dollop of Hollandaise sauce and serve immediately.

Serves 4.

Harper's Weekly illustration, March 4, 1884.

"I DEMAND THE SURRENDER OF SYLVESTER CANNON"

Sylvester Cannon was a dredge boat captain. To show complete contempt for the Oyster Navy, he and his crew fired warning shots at the police before quickly commencing the dredging on forbidden oyster beds. Not surprisingly, Sly—alas, not living up to his nickname—landed in jail.

OYSTERS RON WHITE

My friend Ron White has spent countless hours in the Crab Lab kitchen. Ron and I agree that simple is best, and when you use fresh oysters and fresh garden herbs and vegetables, you can make the most delicious treats.

12	**oysters in shells**
	rock salt
1	**medium tomato, peeled and diced**
1	**clove garlic, minced**
1	**teaspoon basil**
2	**tablespoons olive oil**
½	**cup grated Asiago cheese**
	salt and pepper

Shuck the oysters, leaving the meat in the deep shells and discarding the top shells and liquor. Line a baking pan with about half an inch of rock salt to hold the oyster shells upright and set the deep shells in the salt.

In a small bowl, combine the tomato, garlic, basil, olive oil, and salt and pepper to taste. Top each oyster with a teaspoonful of the tomato mixture and sprinkle with cheese. Bake at 360°F for 10 minutes or until bubbly. Serve on warm plates lined with rock salt.

Serves 2.

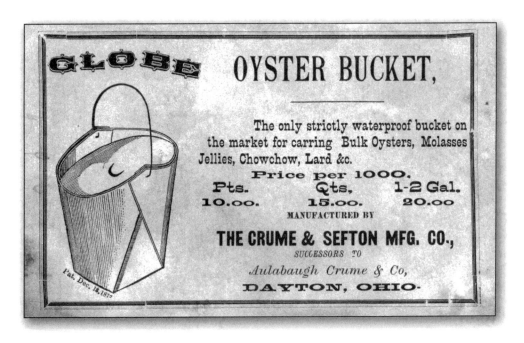

I've probably carried home about 50 gallons of Chinese food in these waterproof buckets and never once thought of where they were made. This trade card is dated December 18, 1872.

OYSTERS HITCHCOCK

The great thing about compound butters is that there are many variations. For garlic butter, omit the lemon and parsley and add 6 cloves of garlic. For herb butter, omit the lemon juice and add 1 level tablespoon of chopped fresh tarragon and chervil.

- 1 **pound unsalted butter**
- 4 **tablespoons chopped fresh parsley**
  salt and pepper to taste
- 3 **tablespoons freshly squeezed lemon juice**

Cut butter into fingernail-size pieces. Place in a mixing bowl and beat with a wooden sppon until soft and fluffy. Beat in the parsley and a dash of salt and pepper. Beat in the lemon juice a few drops at a time. Spread the butter onto a sheet of waxed paper, top with another piece, and roll with a rolling pin until the butter is about the thickness of a 50-cent piece. Seal the ends and chill or freeze.

Top oysters on the half-shell with butter slices and broil until bubbly.

Serves a crowd.

Currier & Ives during the late 1800s produced many signs for retail businesses. This trading card could very well have been designed by them.

OYSTERS CUCKOLD CREEK-STYLE

My friend Cookie Benner, who came up with this recipe, explains: "I know just what you are going to say: That two sticks of butter are just too much. Well, a pound of fettuccine is a lot of pasta and you'll need butter and oil to make the recipe work." She's right. Don't skimp.

OYSTERS

24 oysters in shells
½ pound bacon cut in 1-inch pieces
1 jar (16 ounces) medium salsa
1 bag (32 ounces) shredded mozzarella
    cheese
    lemon wedges

PASTA

1 pound fettuccine
2 sticks butter
½ cup olive oil
2 tablespoons garlic salt
2 tablespoons parsley flakes or chopped
    fresh parsley
½ teaspoon Italian seasoning
    salt and pepper
    Parmigiano-Reggiano cheese

Oysters: Shuck oysters, discarding oyster liquor and top shells and retaining deep shells. Place each oyster in its deep shell and top with 1 teaspoon of salsa, 1 teaspoon of mozzarella cheese, and 1 piece of bacon. Broil until the bacon curls and the cheese starts to brown.

Pasta: Cook fettuccine according to package directions and drain. In a microwave-safe bowl, combine the butter, olive oil, garlic salt, parsley, and Italian seasoning and melt in microwave. Pour over the pasta and mix well. Add salt and pepper to taste.

*T*his penny postcard was dated June 9, 1909—a great year for oysters. And I think I've actually shot pool with this character in the picture, down at the Crisfield VFW hall.

Assembly: Arrange 6 oysters around the outside of each plate and place the pasta in the center. Serve with lemon wedges and Parmigiano-Reggiano cheese. Add a garden salad and enjoy!

Serves 4.

I've inside information

SUSIE'S SELECTS

These selects are simply a little triumph. They make a superlative luncheon dish or a late-evening supper, especially when a crisp green salad and a chilled glass of chardonnay are added for optimum effect.

24   **oysters in shells**
     rock salt
 4   **roma tomatoes, peeled and diced**
 4   **cloves garlic, minced**
 2   **tablespoon fresh herbs (a mix of thyme,**
     parsley, and oregano)
½   **cup grated Parmigiano-Reggiano cheese**
     salt and pepper

Shuck the oysters, leaving the meat in the deep shells and discarding the top shells and liquor. Line a baking pan with about half an inch of rock salt to hold the oyster shells upright and set the deep shells in the salt.

In a small bowl, combine the tomato, garlic, herbs, olive oil, and salt and pepper to taste. Top each oyster with a teaspoonful of the tomato mixture and sprinkle with cheese. Bake at 360°F for 10 minutes or until bubbly. Serve on warm plates lined with rock salt.

Serves 4.

This penny postcard advertisement is one I purchased in an antiques shop a couple of years ago for eight bucks. Approximately 138 beers, 20 bushels and many months later, and I still haven't found Buchanan's.

CHAPTER 7
The Town the Oyster Built
(A History of Crisfield, Maryland)

OYSTERS POCOMOKE SOUND

*"Oysters down in Oyster Bay do it
Let's do it—Let's fall in love."*

—COLE PORTER

¾ cup beer
4 tablespoons butter
½ cup chopped fresh parsley
½ cup chopped onions
4 cloves garlic, minced
1 can (8 ounces) mushrooms, drained and chopped
1 cup heavy cream
½ teaspoon salt
½ teaspoon freshly ground black pepper
1 pound cooked shrimp, chopped in pieces at least ¼ inch long
36 oysters in shells
rock salt
2 tablespoons grated cheddar cheese
2 lemons cut in wedges

Open the beer, take a swig, and set the rest aside.

In a skillet, melt the butter and sauté the parsley, onions, and garlic for 2 to 3 minutes. Then add the mushrooms, the beer, cream, salt, and pepper. Simmer for 10 minutes and then add the chopped shrimp. Simmer for another 5 minutes.

Shuck the oysters, reserving the oyster liquor and the deep bottom shells. Arrange the shells in a bed of rock salt and place an oyster in each. Spoon about ½ teaspoon oyster liquor over each oyster, then broil them for about 2 minutes. Remove them from the broiler and fill them with sauce. Sprinkle a little cheddar cheese on top of each shell and return them to the broiler for 5 minutes. Serve with a wedge of lemon. If there's any beer left, drink it.

Serves 6.

Courtesy of Tighty Mister Collection.

OLD CUSTOM HOUSE ON THE CITY DOCK 1900
FOOT OF BROAD STREET

There's a part of me that would love to have been around during the thrilling days of yesteryear, jus' sittin' out in front of the old custom house, maybe catchin' a ride on one of the workboats, maybe slurpin' an oyster or two. It's worth noting that part of this building is still standing. Guess what it is. Yep, an oyster-packing house.

144

BOAT HARBOR OYSTER HASH

Hash is as old as the harbor itself here in Crisfield. Best described as a dish of finely chopped meat and vegetable (usually potato), the most popular variation is made with corned beef. But this version, with chopped ham and oysters, is a classic in its own right.

    2   tablespoons bacon fat for sautéeing
    ½   pound cooked country ham, cubed
    1   pint oysters and liquor
    2   cups water, or more
    2   cups white cornmeal
         salt and pepper

Sauté ham in bacon fat until it browns lightly; set aside.

Drain the oysters, reserving the oyster liquor, and chop the oysters coarsely. In a heavy skillet, warm the oysters in their liquor just until their edges curl. Add the water and salt and pepper to taste. Gradually stir in the cornmeal and cook, stirring constantly, over very low heat for 10 minutes, or until thickened. If the mush thickens too much, add a little more water. Stir in the ham and serve hot.

Serves 8.

Pictured here is the Crisfield harbor as it appeared in winter 1958. Of interest are the three boats with "draketail" sterns—the ones that "rainbow" out wider at the bottom than at the top. This elegant and rare design feature was first seen on Chesapeake work boats from Hooper Island before the turn of the last century.

Photograph by Scorchy Tawes.

MARYLAND-STYLE PICKLED OYSTERS

Pickling spices vary, but are often a blend of dill, cloves, and salt. My favorite foods to pickle are shrimp and oysters. The blend can differ greatly according to the manufacturer and the ingredients. My advice is to sample several and use the one you like best.

2	**cups white wine**
1	**quart plus 1 cup white vinegar**
2	**tablespoons sugar**
3	**tablespoons mixed pickling spice**
2	**medium carrots, thinly sliced**
1	**medium onion, thinly sliced**
3	**ribs celery, thinly sliced**
½	**teaspoon salt**
1	**quart oysters, drained**
	chopped parsley for garnishing

Combine the wine, 1 quart of the vinegar, sugar, pickling spice, carrot, onion, and celery, and boil for 4 minutes. Strain the vegetables out and discard; reserve the liquid.

In another pot, combine 1 cup vinegar, the salt, and the oysters and let stand for 10 minutes. Bring to a boil and simmer for 3 minutes, and then skim the top. As soon as the oysters' edges begin to curl, strain the oysters from the liquid and drop them into the wine-vinegar mixture. Store, refrigerated, for at least 12 hours or up to 2 weeks.

Serve well chilled and sprinkle with chopped parsley.

Serves 8.

UNLOADING OYSTERS, CRISFIELD, MD.

Crisfield, Maryland is a town that literally rose from the sea. Most of today's downtown was once navigable water as a tributary of the Chesapeake Bay. During the heyday of the commercial oyster harvest, oyster shells were considered to have no value, and millions upon millions were dumped overboard. As the marsh filled in, the oyster houses moved seaward. Note the piles of oyster shells in this photograph.

PEGGY NECK OYSTERS IN A BISCUIT

Golden brown biscuits on the table can make even the most humble meal special. Perfect biscuits are easy to make. The secret is in the mixing (don't stir too much, or they'll get tough and dense). Of course, stuffing them with oysters makes biscuits even better.

1	**pint oysters and liquor**
24	**biscuits**
1	**stick butter, softened**
1	**teaspoon seafood seasoning**
	paprika

Drain oysters and discard oyster liquor. Split the biscuits and hollow out the centers. Thoroughly mix the butter and seasoning and spread liberally on the biscuits. Place one oyster on each biscuit and sprinkle paprika on top. Broil in the lowest section of the broiler until the edges of the oysters curl, about 4 minutes. Top with the other half of the biscuit. Serve at once.

Makes 24 biscuits.

Courtesy of Tighty Mister Collection.

LIME PLANT, "ONE MILLION BUSHELS OF OYSTER SHELLS" 1943

It wasn't long before someone realized that oyster shells were good for other things besides protecting future fried oysters. They're a valuable raw material for the production of lime and chicken feed, among other things. This postcard from 1943 shows one million bushels worth of shells.

The Oyster
The oyster's a confusing suitor;
It's masc., and fem.,
And even neuter.
But whether husband,
Pal, or wife,
It leads a soothing
Sort of life.
I'd like to be
An oyster, say,
In August, June,
July, or May.
—OGDEN NASH

GIBSON STORE SCALLOPED OYSTERS

This dish is very popular with my friends who stop by the Crab Lab for a visit. It's a little unusual but easy to prepare, and will delight your guests, too.

1	**pint oysters and liquor**
2	**cups coarse cracker crumbs**
½	**cup butter, melted**
½	**teaspoon salt**
⅛	**teaspoon pepper**
¼	**teaspoon Worcestershire sauce**
1	**cup milk**

Drain the oysters and discard the oyster liquor. Combine the cracker crumbs, butter, salt, and pepper. Reserve a third of this mixture for topping. Place another third in a lightly-oiled 1-quart baking dish and cover with half the oysters. Repeat these two layers. Add the Worcestershire sauce to the milk and pour it over the casserole. Top with the reserved crumb mixture. Bake at 350°F for 30 minutes or until thoroughly heated.

Serves 6.

Tighty Mister Collection.

Buy boat: a boat involved with the purchase of oysters—right out at the oyster-harvesting grounds—from tongers and dredgers, rushing the purchase to market in the cities and towns around the Bay. This photo shows such a vessel in port beside the W. E. Gibson Seafood packing plant.

PUPPY HOLE CREAMED OYSTERS

Three key ingredients—oysters, heavy cream, and freshly grated nutmeg—are the secrets to this rich and luscious luncheon special. I serve it with a mixed garden salad and a glass of chilled chardonnay. Cheers!

1 **pint oysters and liquor**
   bottled clam juice
2 **tablespoons butter plus additional for**
   buttering toast points
2 **tablespoons all-purpose flour**
¼ **cup heavy cream**
   salt and freshly ground black pepper
1 **teaspoon Worcestershire sauce**
½ **teaspoon freshly grated nutmeg**
⅛ **teaspoon cayenne pepper**
   toast points
1 **tablespoon chopped fresh parsley**

Drain the oysters and reserve the oyster liquor. To the oyster liquor, add enough clam juice to make 1 cup.

In a saucepan, heat the butter and whisk inn the flour. When blended and smooth, add the oyster liquor mixture, whisking rapidly. When blended and smooth, add the cream and stir. Add the salt, pepper, Worcestershire sauce, nutmeg, and cayenne pepper. Add the oysters and cook over gentle heat until the edges curl.

Butter the toast points while hot and top with the oyster mixture. Sprinkle each serving with parsley.

Serves 4.

For much of the 20th century, the wide waters of Pocomoke and Tangier Sounds provided hundreds of watermen thousands of acres of some of the finest oyster grounds in the world. And working within a stone's throw of Crisfield, these watermen could easily get their catch to market.

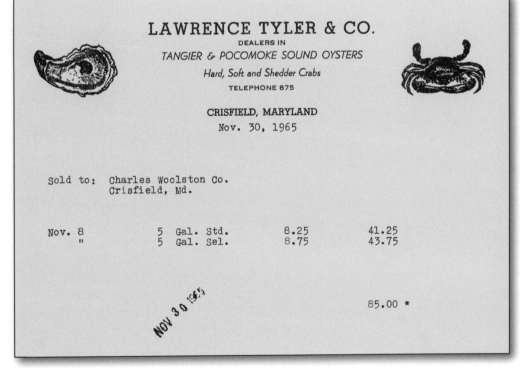

LAWRENCE TYLER & CO.
DEALERS IN
TANGIER & POCOMOKE SOUND OYSTERS
Hard, Soft and Shedder Crabs
TELEPHONE 875

CRISFIELD, MARYLAND
Nov. 30, 1965

Sold to: Charles Woolston Co.
          Crisfield, Md.

Nov. 8   5 Gal. Std.   8.25   41.25
    "   5 Gal. Sel.   8.75   43.75

                                          85.00 *

NOV 30 1965

OLD ISLAND BAKED OYSTERS

If you're standing at the end of City Dock here in Crisfield, you can still see the brick chimney jutting up from Old Island out in the harbor. That used to be part of the L.E.P. Dennis Fish Fertilizer Factory. If you stand at the end of my dining room table, you can often see the following dish bubbling away in my oven. Use a well-seasoned cast iron pan, a cake pan or a casserole dish. But be sure to grease whatever type of cookware you choose.

4 **tablespoons butter**
1 **cup fresh white breadcrumbs**
1 **tablespoon finely chopped garlic**
2 **tablespoons finely chopped fresh parsley**
1 **pint oysters and liquor**
3 **tablespoons Parmigiano-Reggiano cheese**

In a small pan, melt 2 tablespoons of the butter and add breadcrumbs and garlic. Sauté until golden brown, 2 to 3 minutes. Stir in the parsley. Spread two-thirds of the crumb mixture in a buttered baking dish.

Drain the oysters, discard oyster liquor, and arrange them in one layer on top of the crumb mixture. Mix the rest of the breadcrumbs with the Parmigiano-Reggiano cheese and spread this mixture over the oysters. Cut the remaining 2 tablespoons of butter into tiny pieces and dot on top of the casserole. Bake at 450°F until bubbly.

Serves 4.

At certain remote parts of the Eastern Shore, you can still see wooden structures that watermen once built to keep a lookout on their oyster beds. This picture from Frank Leslie's Illustrated Newspaper *for the week ending January 9, 1886 shows how bad the Oyster Wars got between the Marylanders and Virginians. Here, a guard boat stands watch over some private oyster beds.*
The title: "Midnight Alarm."

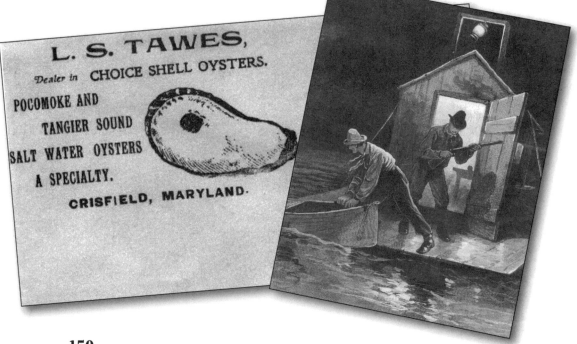

CRISFIELD HARBOR SAUTÉED OYSTERS

Cumin is a plant of the carrot family whose small, pungent, crescent-shaped seeds are widely used in Middle Eastern cookery. How it ended up in this oyster dish in Crisfield is beyond me. But I'm glad it did. Just try it. The nutty flavor is beyond belief.

6	tablespoons butter
1	pound medium mushrooms, sliced
1	quart oysters and liquor
6	garlic cloves, minced
1½	teaspoons ground cumin
⅔	cup dry white wine

Use 2 large skillets for this quick sauté. Divide the butter between the pans and lightly brown it over medium-high heat. Then toss the mushrooms in and cook them until they develop a golden tinge. Meanwhile, drain the oysters and discard the oyster liquor. Put the oysters in a bowl and coat them well with the garlic and cumin. Add the oysters to the hot pans and shake and toss until the edges of the oysters curl.

When the oysters are cooked, add wine to each pan and let the juices bubble up and burn off the wine's alcohol for a minute or so. Serve hot.

Serves 8.

L. S. Tawes was not only a Crisfield oyster packer, he was also known as Captain Leonard S. Tawes. He began his maritime career at the age of 15 as a cook on a Chesapeake Bay oyster-dredging pungy (a type of schooner). Later he advanced from the smaller Bay craft and became part owner and captain of the three-masted schooner City of Baltimore. *Is that how the cumin got to Crisfield?*

.... Gals. Med. .... Gal. Standards. .... Gal. Selects.

FOR.

FROM

L. S. TAWES,
DEALER IN
CHOICE SHELL OYSTERS,
Pocomoke and Tangier Sound Salt
Water Oysters a Specialty.
CRISFIELD, - MARYLAND

151

MARION STATION CREAMED OYSTERS

The combination of oysters and cream in the easy-to-prepare dish is a surefire delight. The cheese and breadcrumbs help to hold it together. The end effect is a velvety, chowder-like dish.

6   slices white bread, buttered and cubed
4   ounces sharp cheddar cheese, shredded
1   pint oysters and liquor
2   eggs
2   tablespoons grated yellow onion
¼   cup finely chopped green onion
1   teaspoon salt
¼   teaspoon black pepper
2¾ cups heavy cream
    dash of Tabasco sauce
3   tablespoons butter plus additional for
    greasing casserole dish

Butter a 2-quart casserole dish. Place half of the bread cubes in the dish and add the grated cheese on top.

Drain the oysters and discard the oyster liquor. Distribute the oysters on top of the cheese and top with the remaining bread cubes.

In a bowl, beat together the eggs, yellow and green onions, salt, pepper, milk, and Tabasco sauce. Pour over the casserole. Dot the top with butter and bake for 1¼ hours at 325°F.

Serves 6.

Courtesy of Tighty Mister Collection.

THE DOCKS   1870

During the Civil War, the business of shucking and canning oysters was founded in Baltimore. To supply those oysters, the vessel owners along the Bay dredged with patented winders and dredges. With the Tangier and Pocomoke Sound oyster beds being nearby, the railroad was extended to the docks in Crisfield, Maryland. The first train ran on November 4, 1866. The rest is history. In its heyday, three trains a day left Crisfield on a regular schedule. Most, were loaded with seafood headed for the markets of Philadelphia and New York.

JANES ISLAND OYSTER DIP

Here's a dip I guarantee you're gonna love whether you love oysters or not, and it goes great with crackers, crostini, or fresh broccoli, cauliflower, carrots, or celery.

1   **pint oysters and liquor**
1   **cup dry white wine**
1   **cup cream cheese, softened**
3   **cups sour cream**
¼   **cup finely chopped green onions**
2   **tablespoons finely chopped fresh thyme**
2   **tablespoons finely chopped fresh parsley**
2   **tablespoons chopped capers**
1   **teaspoon Tabasco sauce**
    freshly ground black pepper

Drain the oysters and discard the liquor. In a saucepan, bring the wine to a boil. Reduce to a simmer and drop in the oysters. Cook for about 3 minutes, or until the oysters begin to plump. Drain and coarsely chop the oysters.

In a mixing bowl, beat the cream cheese until creamy. Add the sour cream, mixing well. stir in the green onion, thyme, parsley, and capers, mixing well. Gently fold in the oysters. Season to taste with Tabasco sauce and black pepper. Transfer to a serving bowl.

Serves 10 to 20.

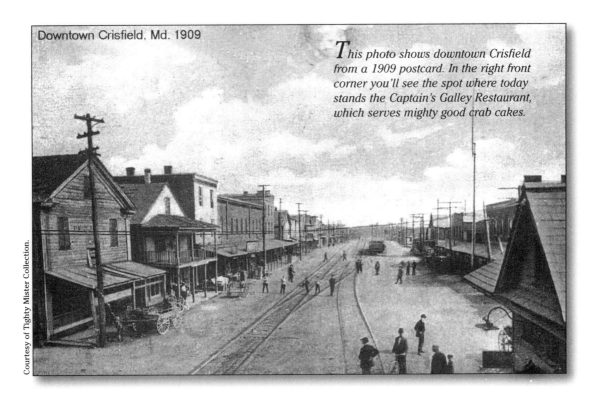

Downtown Crisfield, Md. 1909

This photo shows downtown Crisfield from a 1909 postcard. In the right front corner you'll see the spot where today stands the Captain's Galley Restaurant, which serves mighty good crab cakes.

Courtesy of Tighty Mister Collection.

153

CARVEL HALL OYSTER SALAD

For a special presentation, compose a colorful salad on individual plates or on a large platter. Make it the diners' choice whether to nibble the elements separately or mix them together. Watch out for the guest who just picks the oysters off the top, though. He should be severely punished!

20	oysters in shells
½	cup olive oil
2	tablespoons fresh lime juice
¼	cup chopped green pepper
¼	cup chopped red pepper
¼	cup chopped yellow pepper
1	scallion, finely chopped (including green top)
1	small clove garlic, minced
1	teaspoon Dijon mustard
1	tablespoon chopped fresh parsley
1	teaspoon chopped fresh dill
¼	teaspoon crumbled dried rosemary
	salt and freshly ground black pepper
	radicchio and endive leaves

Shuck the oysters, reserving the oyster liquor and discarding the shells. In a small saucepan, combine the oysters and their liquor and cook over medium-low heat just until the edges curl, about 3 minutes.

In a bowl, whisk together the oil, lime juice, chopped peppers, scallion, garlic, mustard, parsley, dill, rosemary, and salt and pepper to taste. Stir in the oysters. Cover and refrigerate overnight.

Arrange the radicchio and endive on serving plates and top with the oyster salad.

Serves 4.

T ake a look at this invoice and the cost for five gallons of Chincoteague salt oysters back on April 12, 1940. Just last week I bought one gallon for $50. This is what keeps me up at night.

OYSTER SALAD WITH JERSEY ISLAND DRESSING

Extra virgin olive oil, a quality vinegar (either wine, berry, rice, or herbed) and a carefully selected mustard like a "do-john" are some of the essentials for this Jersey Island oyster salad.

1 quart oysters and liquor
2 heads of crisp lettuce
3 egg yolks
1 teaspoon prepared mustard
1 teaspoon salt
3 tablespoons olive oil
2 tablespoons vinegar
  black pepper
  cayenne pepper

In a large saucepan, bring the oysters to a boil in their own liquor. Drain and set aside to cool. Arrange lettuce leaves in a salad bowl. Turn the oysters into the center of the bowl.

To make the dressing, beat together the egg yolks, mustard, and salt until they begin to thicken. Gradually add the olive oil, as in making mayonnaise, until the mixture thickens. Beat in the vinegar and serve on the oyster salad.

Serves 8.

During the early days of the oyster industry here on the Bay, trade cards like this one, from Geo. A. Christy & Sons, were required of any small oyster company worth its salt.

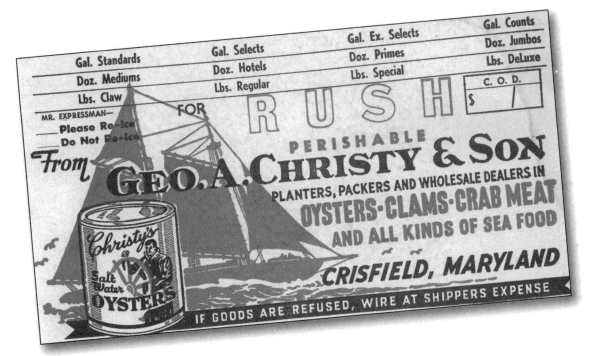

ARCADE THEATER GRILLED OYSTERS

Savory Smithfield ham is one of the things that makes living in Bay country such an exciting experience. A little Smithfield ham, some Chesapeake oysters, and a seat out back overlooking the water. All we need now is some cold chardonnay and a good friend.

12	large oysters in shells
	black pepper
4	tablespoons melted butter
	breadcrumbs
4	slices bread
4	slices Smithfield ham
1	cup light cream sauce with chopped celery
	lemon
	parsley

Shuck the oysters and discard shells and oyster liquor. Dry the oysters on paper towels, sprinkle them with pepper, dip them first in butter and then in breadcrumbs, and broil quickly to a light golden color.

Toast the bread. In a skillet, pan-fry the ham in water until limp, about 1 minute per side. Place a slice of ham on each piece of toast. Then place 3 oysters on each piece of ham, garnish with lemon and parsley, and pour cream sauce around each piece of toast.

Serves 2.

An oyster shucker stands on a raised box to protect feet and clothing from Bay water, oyster liquor, mud, and debris. The shucker quickly extracts the bivalves and flicks them into the stainless steel gallon buckets. The shucking station pictured below is now part of the Crisfield Heritage Foundation exhibit, which you can visit when you're in town.

CITY DOCK OYSTER FRICASSEE

A fricassee is a type of stew based on a meat stock. This dish, a unique variation, is best when served with wild rice, glazed carrots and a tossed spinach salad.

2 **sticks butter**
2 **quarts oysters**
1 **cup heavy cream**
3 **tablespoon all-purpose flour**
1 **teaspoon black pepper**
   salt
3 **egg yolks, well beaten**
   buttered toast

In a large saucepan, let the butter come to a sizzle. Add the oysters and let them cook until plump. Remove the pan from the heat, add the flour and stir to incorporate. Then add cream, pepper, and salt to taste. Over heat once more, let the mixture come to a boil and then quickly stir in the egg yolks. Remove from heat at once and serve on a platter of buttered toast.

Serves 10.

Make no mistake: opening oysters is an art. While the professional shuckers make it look easy, that's only because they've done it thousands of times and have sharpened their skills. A top-notch shucker can open as many as 12 gallons of oysters in an eight-hour day.

157

OYSTERS PARMESAN

Whoever first melted cheese over toast should get a medal. For me, it's not only one of the first things I ever cooked, but now, more than 60 years later, I am still using the combination—just in more sophisticated ways.

1   **pint oysters and liquor**
2   **tablespoons chopped onion**
2   **cups milk, divided**
3   **tablespoons butter**
4   **tablespoons all-purpose flour**
½   **teaspoon salt**
    dash of pepper
½   **teaspoon celery salt**
½   **cup grated Parmigiano-Reggiano cheese**
2   **teaspoons chopped parsley**
6   **hard rolls**
    paprika

Drain the oysters and discard the liquor. In a saucepan, combine the oysters, the onion, and 1 cup of the milk. Cook over medium heat for 15 minutes. In another saucepan, melt the butter and blend in the flour, salt, pepper, and celery salt. Add the remaining 1 cup milk and cook until thick, stirring constantly. Add the Parmigiano-Reggiano, cheese, and parsley. Combine the cheese sauce with the oyster mixture and cook for 5 minutes more. Serve hot over split hard rolls. Sprinkle paprika over each serving.

Serves 6.

Railroad records show that on December 19, 1920, the largest single-day shipment of oysters left Crisfield aboard a train pulling 18 boxcar loads of oysters, consisting of 60,000 gallons, which came from some 80,000 bushels of fresh bivalves shucked at the Crisfield waterfront. That's a lot of shucking.

CAP'N OY

 There is something comforting about the ease and simplicity of preparing oysters this way. The mushroom cradles the succulent oyster as naturally as the oyster shell does.

24 large fresh mushroom caps
4 tablespoons butter plus additional for greasing cookie sheet
6 green onions, finely chopped
½ sweet red pepper in julienne strips
24 small Bay oysters
melted butter
salt

Sauté the mushroom crowns gently in the 4 tablespoons of butter for 3 minutes, stirring carefully so caps do not break. Remove the caps from the pan and place them on a greased cookie sheet hollow side up.

Sauté the onions in the same pan until limp. Place about ¼ teaspoon sautéed onions in each mushroom cap. Sauté the pepper strips in the same pan until limp and set aside.

Shuck the oysters and discard oyster liquor and shells. Dip the oysters in the melted butter and place an oyster atop the onions in each mushroom cap. Sprinkle lightly with salt. Heat under the broiler until the edges of the oysters start to curl. Serve at once, garnished with the red pepper strips.

Serves a crowd.

Pictured here is Chippie Dize, one of Crisfield's finest shuckers. I caught up with him at the Southern Connection Plant #3. When I asked him to "hold 'em up high," he said, "Man, they're big oysters. I can't lift 'em that high!" Understood, Chippie, understood.

OYSTERS KIE TYLER

During the oyster heydays of the 20th century, Crisfield had its share of characters with hearts of gold. None, however, topped Kie Tyler, who passed away in 2002. Kie was a waterman, a personal hero and a flat-out wonderful guy. Thanks, Kie, for all the oysters you shucked and the crabs you caught for our table. We'll miss ya.

36	oysters in shells
1	cup mayonnaise
½	cup chili sauce
6	tablespoons horseradish
3	teaspoons lemon juice
1½	teaspoons dry mustard
1	cups fresh breadcrumbs
½	teaspoon paprika

Shuck oysters, discarding oyster liquor and reserving deep shells.

Place shells on baking pans and place an oyster on each shell.

In a bowl, mix well the mayonnaise, chili sauce, horseradish, lemon juice, mustard, breadcrumbs, and paprika. Cover each oyster generously with this mixture. Broil or bake at 400°F for approximately 10 minutes.

Serves 4 to 6.

After oysters are shucked, they are weighted and placed on the skimming board. The worker then gently skims the oysters to remove shells, debris and any extra oyster liquor, preparing them for market.

CANAL ROAD OYSTER BAKE

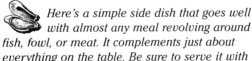 *Here's a simple side dish that goes well with almost any meal revolving around fish, fowl, or meat. It complements just about everything on the table. Be sure to serve it with ice-cold Chardonnay if you're using it as an appetizer.*

2	tablespoons butter
1	large onion, chopped
1	quart oysters and liquor
¼	cup light cream
6	slices bacon, fried and crumbled
½	teaspoon dried dill weed
2	tablespoons grated Parmigiano-Reggiano cheese
4	tablespoons grated cheddar cheese
2	tablespoons butter
	salt and pepper
	lemon slices

In a small pan, melt the butter and sauté the onion until translucent but not browned.

Spread the onions over the bottom of a buttered 9-by-12-inch baking dish. Drain the oysters, discarding the oyster liquor, and spread them over the onions. Pour the cream over the oysters and sprinkle with the crumbled bacon.

Combine the Parmigiano-Reggiano and cheddar cheeses with the dill weed and sprinkle over the oysters. Dot with butter and add salt and pepper to taste.

Bake at 450°F for 8 to 10 minutes, or until lightly browned. Serve with lemon slices.

Serves 8.

After the oysters are "skimmed"—washed and sorted—the next job is to fill the gallon containers and get the product ready for market. Once the gallon containers are full, they are ready for retailing.

DOWN NECKER STIR FRY

 *Stir-frying oysters has been with us for generations, highlighted with garlic, ginger and onions, which add both flavor and fragrance.*

1	tablespoon cornstarch
1	tablespoon water
1½	tablespoons oil
2	cloves garlic, minced
2	tablespoons chopped green onion
1	tablespoon minced fresh, peeled ginger
1	pint oysters and liquor
½	cup orange juice
2	tablespoons soy sauce

Mix the cornstarch with water in a small bowl and set aside. Heat the oil in a wok. Add garlic, onion, and ginger, and stir-fry for approximately 1 minute. Drain the oysters and add them to the wok along with the orange juice and soy sauce. Stir-fry for an additional 60 seconds.

Add the cornstarch mixture and cook until the sauce just starts to thicken, about 1 minute more. Serve immediately with rice.

Serves 4.

Inside the shucking houses, oyster shells are shoveled onto conveyor belts, which carry them outside to giant piles. Seagulls always perch nearby, waiting for their morsels of fresh lunch . . . confirming the rumor: I do own a seagull costume.

OYSTERS WARD BROS.

I named this recipe for the world-famous Lem and Steve Ward, who are known for their fine duck-decoy carvings. They wanted to "counterfeit" nature and create a bird that looked more real than the real thing. Their old workshop is now a museum here in Crisfield. You can share in their creative impulse by creating this dish— again and again.

	rock salt
3	tablespoons butter
¼	cup finely chopped green onions
¼	cup all-purpose flour
¾	cup fish stock
3	tablespoons white wine
¼	teaspoon salt
	dash of cayenne pepper
1	egg yolk, beaten
½	cup finely chopped cooked, peeled, and deveined shrimp
½	cup finely chopped mushrooms
¼	cup chopped pimento
1	teaspoon Worcestershire sauce
2	teaspoons chopped fresh parsley
12	oysters in shells
	pimento strips

Put a half-inch layer of rock salt in 2 pie pans; place in a hot oven to preheat the salt.

In a saucepan, melt the butter and sauté the onion. Blend in the flour; cook, stirring constantly, for about 5 minutes. Do not brown. Remove from heat and stir in the fish stock, wine, salt, and cayenne pepper. Mix well.

Blend a small amount of this hot mixture into the egg yolk and then stir the egg yolk back into the remaining hot mixture. Add the shrimp, mushrooms, chopped pimento, Worcestershire sauce, and parsley; cook over low heat for about 15 minutes.

Shuck the oysters, discarding the liquor and top shells and retaining the deep shells. Arrange 6 shells in each pie pan and place an oyster in each shell. Spoon sauce over each oyster. Bake at 350° for 10 to 15 minutes or until the edges of the oysters begin to curl.

Garnish with pimento strips.

Serves 2.

Crisfield has come a long way from the time the Indians camped and canoed along the banks of Pocomoke Sound and the Annemessex River. One thing that hasn't changed is payday. And you'd better not be late to the window!

NEW FERRY OYSTER SURPRISE

*I won't be surprised if you fall in love
with Crisfield after spending a few
days—and nights, most importantly—here. You'll
also fall in love with this devilish oyster dish.*

36	oysters in shells
1	tablespoon butter
2	tablespoons all-purpose flour
½	pint heavy cream
2	egg yolks, beaten
1	tablespoons finely chopped fresh parsley
1	bay leaf, chopped fine
1	pinch mace
1	sprig thyme, finely chopped
3	sprigs parsley
	salt and cayenne pepper
	breadcrumbs
	butter
	sprigs of parsley, olives, sliced lemon

Shuck the oysters, reserving the deep shells
and discarding the top shells and liquor. Chop
the oysters. Rub the butter and flour together
with your fingertips until the mixture is
smooth. In a saucepan, heat the cream. When it
comes to a boil, stir in the butter/flour mixture.
Remove from heat and add the egg yolks,
chopped parsley, bay leaf, mace, and thyme.
Add salt and cayenne pepper to taste, and then
add the oysters.

Fill the oyster shells with the oyster mixture
and sprinkle with breadcrumbs; dot with butter
and set in a baking pan. Bake at 375°F until
golden brown.

Garnish with parsley sprigs or asparagus
tips, olives, and lemon slices.

Serves 6.

*C*risfield is so in touch with its past and where
*it's headed that this is the official key to the city,
made up, appropriately enough, of an oyster
knife and a locally made Carvel Hall crab-picking
knife, like the one used by yours truly.*

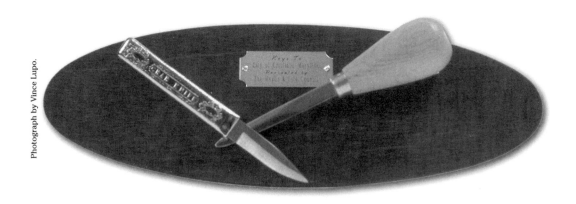

Photograph by Vince Lupo.

CHAPTER 8
Rich as Rockefeller

BEFORE THE STORM OYSTERS ROCKEFELLER

Oysters Rockefeller originated in 1899 at Antoine's, the famous New Orleans restaurant founded by Jules "Antoine" Alciatore. According to legend, the recipe was named when a customer tasting it for the first time said, "This recipe is as rich as Rockefeller."

36	oysters in shells
	rock salt
1½	cups tightly packed fresh spinach
¾	cup tightly packed parsley leaves
¾	cup chopped scallions, including green tops
6	shallots, chopped
3	tablespoons chopped fresh fennel leaves
2	sticks unsalted butter
2	tablespoons anchovy paste
	Tabasco sauce
1	cup fresh breadcrumbs
½	cup anisette
	salt and black pepper

Shuck the oysters, saving and straining the oyster liquor and retaining the deep shells. Scrub and dry the deep shells and arrange them in pans filled with rock salt. Put an oyster in each shell.

Purée the spinach, parsley, scallions, shallots, and fennel in a food processor.

In a saucepan, melt the butter over low heat and cook the vegetables in it for 5 minutes. Stir in the anchovy paste, several dashes of Tabasco sauce, and the breadcrumbs. Cook, stirring, until well mixed and thick. Add oyster liquor or more crumbs to adjust thickness.

Add anisette, salt and pepper to taste. Spread the sauce over the oysters and bake at 450°F for about 5 minutes. Serve at once.

Serves 6.

Photograph by Vince Lupo.

Before the storm, or after the storm, you will find these two guys waiting in line for oysters. That's Buddy Harrison on the left and the author on the right, talking bivalves at Harrison's Chesapeake House on Maryland's Tilghman Island.

TOBACCO TRADERS OYSTERS ROCKEFELLER

Here's a tip: When cooking oysters on the half-shell, place them on a bed of rock salt. This serves two purposes: It keeps them hot after you remove them from the oven, and it keeps them from tipping over and spilling the toppings. If you don't have any rock salt handy, you can crumple some aluminum foil and arrange the shells on top of that before baking.

  2 **boxes (10 ounces each) frozen spinach**
 24 **oysters in shells**
  1 **cup Parmigiano-Reggiano cheese**
1½ **cups mayonnaise**
  6 **strips bacon**

Thaw the spinach in a colander and squeeze out as much of the water as possible. In a bowl, mix the spinach, Parmigiano-Reggiano cheese, and mayonnaise until creamy. The texture should be thick.

Shuck the oysters, discarding oyster liquor and top shells and retaining the deep shells. Put the shells in baking pans and put an oyster in each shell. Top each oyster with enough of the spinach mixture to cover.

Cut the bacon strips in fourths and drape one piece over each oyster. Bake a 350°F for about 20 minutes, or until the bacon is crisp. Serve hot.

Serves 6.

Longtime oyster slurper and reincarnated rogue tobacco trader Rob McBrayer puts down another dozen.

Photograph by Vince Lupo.

167

Follow the Water Oysters Rockefeller

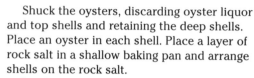 *The most important characteristic of any oyster dish is freshness. After that, size and shape don't tend to be as important as where the oysters come from. Salty Chinco-teagues, Long Island Blue Points, Chesapeakes . . . I love 'em all.*

36	oysters in shells
	rock salt
1	small onion, minced
2	bay leaves, crumbled
½	teaspoon celery salt
⅛	teaspoon cayenne pepper
½	teaspoon salt
2	tablespoons minced fresh parsley
1	cup minced raw spinach
2	sticks butter
½	cup cracker crumbs
1	teaspoon Worcestershire sauce
3	tablespoons sherry
½	cup breadcrumbs
½	cup grated Parmigiano-Reggiano cheese
	lemon wedges

Shuck the oysters, discarding oyster liquor and top shells and retaining the deep shells. Place an oyster in each shell. Place a layer of rock salt in a shallow baking pan and arrange shells on the rock salt.

In a large mixing bowl, combine the onion, bay leaves, celery salt, cayenne pepper, salt, parsley, spinach, and Worcestershire sauce. Mix thoroughly.

In a small saucepan over low heat, melt the butter; remove from heat. Add the cracker crumbs and sherry and mix thoroughly. Add the cracker mixture to the seasonings mixture and mix well.

Top the oysters with the seasoning/cracker crumb mixture. Sprinkle with breadcrumbs and Parmigiano-Reggiano cheese and bake at 400°F for 10 minutes, or until golden brown. Garnish each serving with lemon wedges.

Serves 6.

Photograph by Vince Lupo.

Following the water's rhythms, slurping oysters, drinking beer. It's no wonder that, like the happy bivalve pictured here advertising an old Baltimore pub, I too whistle while I work. I mostly whistle tunes by Cole Porter.

Hard Times Oysters Rockefeller

Anise ("ah-niece") is a parsley-like plant valuable for its seeds, which impart a taste similar to licorice. It is the base for the liqueur anisette, which gives this recipe an elegant lift.

18	oysters in shells
	rock salt
5	tablespoons butter, divided
¼	cup chopped celery
¼	cup chopped green onion
2	tablespoons chopped parsley
1	package (10 ounces) frozen chopped spinach
1	tablespoon anisette
¼	teaspoon salt
¼	cup dry breadcrumbs

Shuck the oysters, discarding the oyster liquor and top shells and retaining the deep shells. Place an oyster in each shell and place the shells on rock salt in shallow baking pans.

In a small saucepan, melt 4 tablespoons of the butter and sauté the celery, green onion, and parsley. Combine these with the spinach in a blender. Add anisette and salt. Blend this mixture until almost pureed.

Top each oyster with the spinach mixture. Melt the last tablespoon of butter and combine it with the breadcrumbs. Sprinkle this mixture over the oysters and bake at 450°F for 10 minutes. Serve immediately from the baking pans (the rock salt will help to keep the oysters warm).

Makes 6 appetizers of 3 oysters each.

Growing up in Southern Maryland, I deemed the Potomac River oysters some of the finest. This tag, which was intended to accompany the sale of a bushel of Potomac oysters, also doubled as a business card and listed cottages for rent. Can you guess the year this tag was printed? (Note the phone numbers—they got two of the early ones.)

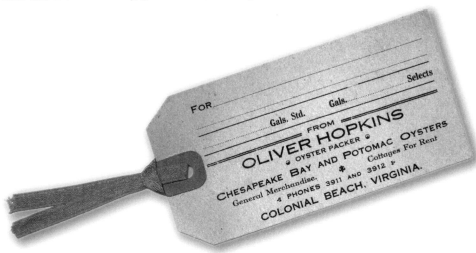

FOGGY RUN OYSTERS ROCKEFELLER

Most good restaurants around the country now have their own versions of Oysters Rockefeller. When I make them, I often vary the ingredients a bit according to what I have on hand. This recipe is a favorite of the Crab Lab taste testers.

36	oysters in shells
	rock salt
1	cup chopped cooked spinach
¼	teaspoon salt
¼	teaspoon black pepper
½	cup melted butter, divided
¼	cup minced onion
1	teaspoon lemon juice
1	teaspoon Accent seasoning
3	tablespoons dry white wine
¾	cup mayonnaise
½	cup half-and-half
1	cup dry bread crumbs
	dash of paprika

Scrub oyster shells under cold running water. Shuck the oysters, discarding the oyster liquor, and place the deep shells on a bed of rock salt. Preheat oven to 375°F. Drain the spinach and blend it with salt, pepper, ¼ cup of the melted butter, and onion. Spoon 1 teaspoon of the spinach mixture into each shell. Place an oyster on top of the spinach and sprinkle with lemon juice and Accent.

Mix the wine with the mayonnaise. When well blended, slowly stir in the half-and-half. Spoon this mixture over the oysters. Mix the bread crumbs with the remaining ¼ cup melted butter and cover the oysters with the buttered crumbs. Sprinkle with paprika. Bake for 20 minutes.

Serves 6.

Woodfield Fish & Oyster Co., located on the West River in Galesville, Maryland, is one of the best when it comes to fresh seafood. I purchased many a crab and oyster from them when I cooked at the Steamboat Landing Restaurant. Boy, that seems like a long time ago, but I can still taste those lovely shellfish.

Photograph by Vince Lupo

NEPTUNE'S DELIGHT OYSTERS ROCKEFELLER

Note to Neptune: Without your dear oyster, we would never have Oysters Rockefeller. Thank you, legendary Lord of the Sea!

36	oysters in shells
	rock salt
¼	pound finely chopped bacon
¼	cup melted butter
½	cup all-purpose flour
½	cup finely chopped green onions
2	cloves garlic, minced
2	cups finely chopped cooked spinach, undrained
½	cup finely chopped fresh parsley
⅛	teaspoon cayenne pepper
¼	cup anisette
	rock salt

Scrub oyster shells under cold running water. Shuck oysters, reserving ½ cup oyster liquor and deep shells.

Put a ½-inch layer of rock salt in each of 6 pie pans and place in 350°F oven to preheat salt. Cook bacon until browned; drain and discard bacon grease. Add butter and flour to bacon and cook, stirring constantly, until golden brown. Add onion, garlic, spinach, parsley, cayenne pepper, oyster liquor, and salt to taste; simmer for 20 minutes. Remove from heat and add anisette, mixing well.

Arrange 6 oyster shells on rock salt in each pie pan. Place an oyster in each shell and top with sauce. Place under the broiler about 6 inches from the source of heat until browned.

Makes 36 appetizers.

COME TO THE
CHESAPEAKE BAY MARITIME MUSEUM
AND CELEBRATE

OYSTER DAY

SATURDAY, NOVEMBER 7TH

11:00 - 3:00

OYSTER DREDGERS ON DISPLAY
SHUCKING DEMONSTRATION
NIPPERING & TONGING FROM THE DOCK
FILM, "HIDDEN TREASURE OF THE BAY"

THE OYSTER HARVEST, presented by George Krantz
OYSTER SHELL SKIPPING CONTEST
ROASTED OYSTERS
For Further Information Call: 745-2916

Oyster Day is a yearly celebration held at the Chesapeake Bay Maritime Museum in St. Michaels, Maryland. Last time I attended, I signed up to take a demo cruise on a Bay workboat. The payoff: A half-dozen of the freshest Miles River oysters I'm ever likely to encounter.

TOLLY POINT ROAD OYSTERS ROCKEFELLER

Oysters Rockefeller has been reinvented so many times over the past one hundred years, it sometimes looks like a whole new dish. That's the case with this excellent version, which features plenty of chopped vegetables, including shallots—a personal favorite.

    2 cups chopped fresh spinach
    ¼ cup finely chopped shallots
    24 oysters in shells
    3 tablespoons melted butter, divided
    3 tablespoons chopped parsley
    3 cloves garlic, minced
       several drops of Tabasco sauce
       dash of pepper
    ¼ cup fine, dry seasoned bread crumbs
       rock salt

In a saucepan, cook spinach and shallots in a small amount of boiling water for 2 to 3 minutes, or until tender. Drain and press out excess moisture.

Scrub oyster shells under cold running water. Shuck the oysters, discarding the oyster liquor and reserving the deep shells. Place each oyster in a shell. Combine the spinach mixture, 2 tablespoons of the melted butter, parsley, garlic, Tabasco sauce, and pepper. Spoon 1 teaspoon onto each oyster.

Toss together bread crumbs and remaining melted butter. Sprinkle over spinach-topped oysters. Fill a shallow baking pan with rock salt to about ½-inch depth. Arrange oysters on the salt and bake at 425°F for 10 to 12 minutes, or until oysters have curled.

Serves 4.

Bluepoints Company of West Sayville, Long Island, created a lot of advertising art, including this piece, whose ad copy reads: "These Sealshipt oysters have the natural sea flavor—the true tang o' the sea. Free from any adulteration or preservation; just fresh, delicious oysters." I'll buy that for a dollar.

DREDGERS AT NIGHT OYSTERS ROCKEFELLER

When you check this recipe's ingredients, you'll think three pounds of greens sounds like a lot. But remember, you'll be using only the leaves of the watercress, and the spinach will cook down significantly.

36	oysters in shells
1	bottle clam broth
2	sticks butter
1	cup all-purpose flour
1	cup minced onions
3	tablespoons anchovy paste
1	tablespoon chopped garlic
	salt and freshly ground black pepper
1½	pounds fresh watercress, washed, patted dry, trimmed, and finely chopped
1½	pounds fresh spinach, washed, patted dry, trimmed, and finely chopped
⅓	cup anisette
	rock salt
½	cup grated Parmigiano-Reggiano cheese
	lemon slivers

Shuck the oysters, saving and straining the oyster liquor, discarding the top shells, and retaining the deep shells. If you don't have 2 cups of oyster liquor, add enough clam broth to make 2 cups.

In a sauté pan over medium heat, melt the butter. Stir in the flour and cook for 4 minutes. Stir in the onions and cook for 2 more minutes. Add the anchovy paste, garlic, watercress, and spinach. Season with salt and pepper and cook for 2 minutes. Stir in the oyster liquor and bring the mixture to a boil. Reduce to a simmer and continue to cook for 10 minutes or until the sauce is thick. Remove from the heat and add the anisette. Add more salt and pepper if needed.

Spread the rock salt evenly over a large sheet pan and arrange the oyster shells on it. Place an oyster in each shell and season each with salt and pepper. Place a heaping spoonful of the filling on top of each oyster and top with grated Parmigiano-Reggiano cheese. Bake at 400°F for about 5 minutes or until the sauce is golden brown and the oysters have curled. Serve on a large platter and garnish with lemon slivers.

Serves 6

At my age, I don't dress up for Halloween anymore. But for this particular Halloween event, I did bother to wear my cleanest T-shirt and least wrinkly blue jeans. The ladies, needless to say, were impressed. "I'm dressed up as an oyster-loving Crisfield resident," I'd tell them.

173

MOTLEY CREW OYSTERS ROCKEFELLER

"While working with my father in 1913 we caught and landed in one day 585 bushels which we sold at 25 cents a bushel and got paid off at 17 cents. This was the largest amount we caught in one day."

—MOTLEY CREWMAN EDWIN BEITZELL, IN HIS BOOK *LIFE ON THE POTOMAC RIVER*

1   **pound spinach**
2   **bunches watercress**
¼   **cup chopped fresh parsley**
2   **sticks unsalted butter**
½   **cup thinly sliced shallots**
¼   **cup chopped celery heart**
1   **teaspoon salt**
1   **teaspoon freshly ground black pepper**
1   **teaspoon fennel seed**
½   **teaspoon cayenne pepper**
⅓   **cup anisette**
48   **oysters in shells**
     rock salt

(Note: The recipe for sauce makes more than you'll need for 48 oysters; freeze half for another occasion.) Wash the spinach and watercress and remove the stalks. Bring a large pot of water to a boil, plunge in the spinach and watercress, let the water return to a boil, and drain the greens in a colander. Rinse them in cold water. After the greens cool, squeeze out all excess moisture and chop them coarsely.

Finely chop the parsley in a food processor. Cut the butter into small chunks and add it to the parsley. Add the greens, shallots, celery, salt, pepper, fennel, cayenne pepper, and anisette and puree. Refrigerate for several hours.

Shuck the oysters, discarding the oyster liquor and the top shells and retaining the deep shells. Lay a bed of rock salt in several oven-proof baking dishes. Place oyster shells in each dish and place an oyster in each shell. Cover each oyster with a tablespoon of sauce. Bake at 475°F for 4 to 5 minutes, or until the sauce bubbles. Serve at once.

Serves 8.

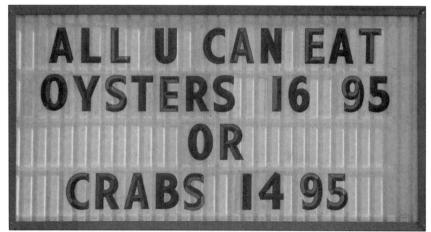

Question: What's all this OR business? I can eat "all I can eat" of both!

DREDGE FLEET OYSTERS ROCKEFELLER

Fennel is a close relative of celery, with a celery-like bulb at its base and a mild, anise-like taste. When using it in this dish, I like to parboil it a couple of minutes, which helps to break down the fennel bulb, imparting more flavor to the dish.

24	**oysters in shells**
	rock salt
6	**tablespoons butter**
½	**cup finely sliced leeks**
½	**cup finely sliced fennel bulb**
¼	**cup finely chopped parsley**
⅓	**cup breadcrumbs**
⅓	**cup anisette**
	salt and freshly ground black pepper
	Tabasco sauce

In a saucepan over medium heat, melt the butter. When it sizzles, add the leeks, fennel and parsley. Cook until tender, about 5 minutes. Remove from the heat and stir in the bread-crumbs and anisette. Transfer the mixture to a food processor and process until finely chopped, about 1 minute. Season to taste with salt, pepper, and Tabasco sauce.

Shuck the oysters, discarding the oyster liquor and the top shells and retaining the deep shells. Place an oyster in each shell. Lay a bed of rock salt in 4 ovenproof baking dishes and place oysters in dishes. Top each oyster with about 1 tablespoon of vegetable mixture and bake at 425°F for about 10 minutes, or until the oysters are heated through and the topping is golden brown.

Photograph by Vince Lupo.

Shucker Eddie Pinder sets the pace at Harrison's Chesapeake House on Tilghman Island, Maryland. This is one of the few guys who can shuck faster than I can slurp.

LOWERING THE TOPSAIL OYSTERS ROCKEFELLER

"The topsail is taken down if the winds get higher than about 20 knots (23 mph—whitecaps). This may call for six or seven hands to keep the topsail from blowing the hell out into the water and taking a couple people with it."

—DECK HAND'S DESCRIPTION OF DAILY CHORES
ABOARD A CHESAPEAKE TOPSAIL SCHOONER

24	oysters in shells
½	cup water
2	teaspoons salt, divided
3	tablespoons butter
1	cup chopped fresh spinach
1	cup chopped fresh turnip greens
2	cups chopped green onions
1	cup chopped green bell pepper
1	cup chopped celery
1	cup chopped fresh parsley
1	tablespoon chopped garlic
1	cup oysters and liquor
1	teaspoon lemon zest
1	teaspoon Tabasco sauce
2	teaspoons anisette
2	teaspoons freshly ground black pepper (ground coarsely)
⅔	cup freshly grated Parmigiano-Reggiano cheese
6	lemon wedges

Shuck the oysters, reserving the oyster liquor, discarding the top shells, and retaining the deep shells. Poach the oysters in the water with 1 teaspoon of salt, simmering over medium heat until the oysters' edges start to curl. Remove them with a slotted spoon and set aside. Discard the poaching liquid.

In a large pan, melt the butter and add the spinach, turnip greens, green onions, green peppers, celery, parsley, and garlic, and sauté until the vegetables are soft and translucent, 8 to 10 minutes. Add the oyster liquor, shucked oysters (not the oysters you set aside), and lemon zest and reduce over medium heat until the liquid is almost gone, about 5 minutes. Add the Tabasco sauce, remaining teaspoon of salt, pepper, anisette, and Parmigiano-Reggiano cheese and transfer the mixture to a food processor. Blend to form a smooth paste.

Place the oyster shells on baking sheets and place a poached oyster in each shell. Spoon the blended mixture on top. Bake at 400°F for 5 minutes, or until the tops start to bubble and brown. Serve with lemon wedges.

Serves 6.

Who says old age affects your memory? I know exactly what I was doing on October 12. What I was doing later that night is a little foggier. But during the day of October 12? Yes, that's still very clear in my mind.

176

GLORY DAYS OYSTERS ROCKEFELLER

 The key to this dish is leaving the oyster liquor in the deeper of the two shells. When the liquor and the butter work together, the results are heavenly on the half-shell.

24	**oysters in shells**
2	**teaspoons chopped fresh parsley**
2	**teaspoons chopped raw spinach**
1	**teaspoon chopped fresh tarragon**
1	**teaspoon chopped fresh chervil**
1	**teaspoon chopped fresh basil**
2	**teaspoons chopped fresh chives**
	salt and freshly ground black pepper
1	**cup fresh breadcrumbs**
1	**stick butter**

Shuck the oysters, leaving as much of the oyster liquor as possible in the deep shells and discarding the top shells. Put the deep shells on a baking sheet and place one oyster in each shell. Sprinkle thickly with the parsley, spinach, tarragon, chervil, basil, and chives, and season with salt and pepper to taste. Cover tops with breadcrumbs and dot with tiny pieces of butter. Bake at 450°F for 5 minutes. Serve hot.

Serves 6.

Here's a 19th-century can label entered by the Thomas J. Myer Company—according to an act of Congress—into the records at the Clerk's Office of the District Court of Maryland.

ON THE WAY OYSTERS ROCKEFELLER

The greenish-brown, comma-shaped aniseed perfumes and flavors this Oysters Rockefeller dish. You'll be surprised at how well the licorice-like flavor accents the oysters.

  1   pound butter, softened
  3   cups very finely chopped cooked
         spinach
 ½   cup finely chopped fresh parsley
  1   cup finely chopped green onion tops
 ¼   cup very finely chopped celery hearts
1½   teaspoons salt
  1   teaspoon freshly ground black pepper
  1   teaspoon dried marjoram
  1   teaspoon dried basil
 ½   teaspoon cayenne pepper
  1   teaspoon freshly ground anise seed
 ½   cup anisette
48   oysters in shells
  8   pie pans with ¼ inch of rock salt

In a mixing bowl, cream the butter lightly. Purée the spinach, parsley, green onion tops, and celery hearts in a blender on high speed for 1 minute. Add the puréed greens to the softened butter. Add the salt, pepper, marjoram, basil, cayenne pepper, anise seed, and anisette, and mix thoroughly.

Place a large piece of wax paper on a flat surface and heap the mixture onto it. Cover with another piece of wax paper and roll out the mixture to a thickness of ¼ inch. Roll up and refrigerate for at least 4 hours.

Shuck the oysters, discarding the oyster liquor and top shells, and retaining the deep shells. Drain the oysters on paper towels. Place an oyster on each shell and set them 6 to a pan on the rock salt. Unroll the chilled Rockefeller sauce and cut it into 48 rectangles about 2 inches by 1¼ inches. Place a rectangle over each oyster and bake at 500°F for 15 minutes, until the sauce bubbles. Serve hot, right from the oven.

Serves 8.

I once ate a bag of steamed crabs while driving the Washington Beltway. But this day, I had two oyster sandwiches. It's much easier to drive when you're not trying to pick backfin.

CARGO BOOM OYSTERS ROCKEFELLER

This recipe is a bit spicy, but it represents a unique addition to the Oysters Rockefeller group. In fact, I could probably just make this sauce and drink it with a straw. It's that tasty.

2   sticks butter
4   ribs celery, chopped
1   pound green onions (about 4 bunches),
        chopped
4   cloves garlic, chopped
2   cups slightly cooked spinach, chopped
        and well drained
4   tablespoons chopped fresh parsley
1   teaspoon salt
⅛   teaspoon cayenne pepper
½   teaspoon ground anise seed
1   tablespoon lemon juice
3   tablespoons Worcestershire sauce
3   tablespoons ketchup
2   ounces anchovy paste
    breadcrumbs
48 oysters in shells
8   pie pans lined with rock salt

In a large saucepan, melt the butter and sauté the celery, green onions, and garlic for 5 minutes. Remove from heat and add spinach, parsley, salt, cayenne pepper, anise seed, lemon juice, Worcestershire sauce, ketchup, and anchovy paste. Mix well. Purée the mixture one quarter at a time in a blender and mix all of the purée together. If the sauce is too moist, add some breadcrumbs.

Shuck and drain the oysters, discarding the oyster liquor and top shells and retaining the deep shells. Place an oyster on each shell and set them 6 to a pan on the rock salt. Bake at 350°F for 10 minutes. Remove the pans from the oven and turn the temperature up to 400°F. Cover each oyster with sauce and return the pans to the oven for 8 minutes, watching them carefully. Brown slightly under the broiler.

Serves 8.

Here's another vintage oyster-can label—origin unknown. I do know there's an island down south, near Hilton Head, called Daufuski. Legend has it that the name is a mongrelized contraction of "The First Key," with said island being the first in a series of islands, or "keys," originally named by the 18th-century Black Americans who first inhabited the area. Who knows if that has anything to do with the oysters?

THICK FOG OYSTERS ROCKEFELLER

There is one universal secret to good cooking: Taste as you go. Add the anisette to this dish, blend, taste, add more if needed, taste, then taste again. Now you're cooking. And eating!

1	stick butter
1	pound chopped fresh spinach
1	cup chopped celery
1	cup chopped green onions
2	cups chopped lettuce
1	cup chopped fresh parsley
¼	cup water
	salt
	cayenne pepper
	Tabasco sauce
3	anchovies, mashed
½	cup seasoned Italian breadcrumbs
2	tablespoons cream
	anisette
36	oysters in shells

In a large pot over medium heat, melt butter and combine the spinach, celery, green onions, lettuce, parsley, water, salt, pepper, and Tabasco sauce. Sauté for 15 minutes, until vegetables are soft and translucent. Add the anchovies and season to taste with salt, cayenne pepper, and Tabasco sauce. Continue cooking for approximately 10 minutes.

Add the breadcrumbs and cream and blend well. Add the anisette and blend. Check the seasonings.

Shuck and drain the oysters, discarding the oyster liquor and top shells and retaining the deep shells. Place an oyster on each shell and place under the broiler for 3 minutes. Remove from the oven and top with the sauce. Bake at 350°F for 20 minutes.

Serves 6.

Chincoteague Island, Virginia, is known for its wild ponies, many of which are rounded up and put into corrals each year to be sold at auction. Apparently, somebody has launched a similar program with Chincoteague's famous salty seaside oysters. Sounds good to me, although I imagine the roundup is a little less dramatic.

Oh, I Remember Oysters Rockefeller

I remember the first Oysters Rockefeller I ever ate: rich, creamy, spirited and rewarding. The experience has led to a lifetime of collecting oyster recipes and artifacts. What I can't seem to remember is where I was at the time and whom I was with. Although I think her name started with an S . . . or was it a T?

36	oysters in shells
	salt
1	lemon, juiced
4	tablespoons butter
4	tablespoons all-purpose flour
2	bunches parsley, stems removed, finely minced
1	bunch green onions, finely minced
3	leeks, white part only, finely chopped
6	ribs celery, strings removed, finely minced
4	tablespoons tomato paste
1½	tablespoons sugar
1	tablespoon vinegar
1	teaspoon ground white pepper
½	teaspoon cayenne pepper
½	cup breadcrumbs
6	small ovenproof baking dishes

Shuck and drain the oysters, reserving the oyster liquor and discarding the shells. Poach the oysters in the oyster liquor, ½ teaspoon salt, and lemon juice until their edges barely begin to curl. Strain the oysters, reserving 1 cup of the liquid, and set aside.

In a saucepan over medium heat, melt the butter. Add the flour and cook for 2 minutes (the flour should not brown). Blend in the reserved oyster poaching liquid and add the parsley, green onions, leeks, and celery. Add the tomato paste, sugar, vinegar, salt, white pepper, and cayenne pepper. Simmer slowly for 1 hour and 15 minutes. Add the breadcrumbs and adjust the seasonings.

Arrange the oysters in individual ovenproof dishes, 6 oysters per dish, and spoon the sauce on top. Bake at 400°F for 12 minutes, or until the sauce is bubbly and beginning to brown.

Serves 6.

In the foreground is a wooden runabout; in the background is a working scow, a flat-bottom boat rigged with a conveyer belt and a hopper. These are the mechanisms often used to drop oyster shells in designated areas of the Bay, to provide reefs and replenish the oyster supply for future generations.

TAKE A LICK OYSTERS ROCKEFELLER DIP

There are times when you want Oysters Rockefeller but all you have is a pint of shucked oysters. No half-shells in sight. Well, no worries. Try this Rockefeller dip. It's simple, delicious and great for entertaining.

36	slices diagonally cut French bread baguette
1	slice white bread
1	pint of oysters and liquor
1	cup coarsely chopped green onions
1	cup coarsely chopped celery
½	cup chopped fresh parsley
3	tablespoons butter
1	package (10 ounces) frozen chopped spinach, thawed and drained

½	cup grated Parmigiano-Reggiano cheese
¼	cup cream cheese
¼	cup evaporated milk
1	tablespoon fresh lemon juice
1	tablespoon Worcestershire sauce
1½	teaspoons anchovy paste
1	turn freshly ground black pepper

Arrange the baguette slices on 2 baking sheets and bake them at 375° until crisp, about 7 minutes.

Place the slice of white bread in a food processor and pulse until coarse crumbs measure ¼ cup.

Poach the oysters in their own liquor and drain, reserving 2 tablespoons of the liquor. When the oysters are cool, chop them.

Place the onions, celery, and parsley in the food processor and process until finely chopped.

In a saucepan, melt the butter over medium-high heat. Add the onion mixture and sauté for 5 minutes or until tender. Add the spinach and cook until it is thoroughly heated. Stir in the oysters, the ¼ cup breadcrumbs, the reserved 2 tablespoons of oyster liquor, the Parmigiano-Reggiano and cream cheeses, the evaporated milk, lemon juice, Worcestershire sauce, anchovy paste, and black pepper. Cook for 2 minutes or until well blended, stirring constantly. Serve with baguette slices.

Serves 18 (serving size is 2 tablespoons dip and 2 baguette slices).

When I saw this handcart loaded with this many oysters, I suddenly felt as rich as a Rockefeller. After heading to the seafood market in search of some similar quarry, I suddenly felt a little less rich.

DANCING WITH THE TIDE ROCKEFELLER

There's no better way to spend a rainy Sunday afternoon than making a batch of these. Indeed, they're "mo' rich than the Brothers Rockefeller"—and with even better taste!

36	oysters in shells
1	stick butter
1	bunch green onions, finely chopped
5	large mushrooms, finely chopped
½	cup all-purpose flour
½	cup dry white wine
3	cups oyster liquor and chicken broth mixed (add enough chicken broth to the oyster liquor to make 3 cups)
3	egg yolks
1	pound finely chopped cooked shrimp salt and finely ground black pepper Tabasco sauce seasoned Italian style breadcrumbs paprika butter

Shuck the oysters, retaining the liquor and deep shells and discarding the top shells. In a saucepan, melt the butter and sauté the onions and mushrooms in it until the onions are soft. Remove from heat and stir in the flour; then add the white wine and stir.

Add the oyster liquor-chicken broth mixture to the onion-mushroom mixture. Return to heat and bring just to a boil, stirring. Simmer for 10 minutes.

In a small bowl, stir the yolks, and then add a little of the simmering liquid, stirring all the time. Pour the yolk mixture into the simmering liquid and cook, stirring, until thickened. Do not boil. Add the shrimp and season to taste with salt, pepper, and Tabasco sauce. Set aside to cool.

Place each oyster on an oyster shell. Cover each oyster with sauce. Sprinkle with breadcrumbs and paprika and moisten with melted butter. Bake at 400°F until bubbly, about 20 minutes.

Serves 6.

*M*cNasby's, located in Annapolis, served as an oyster-packing plant in the winter and a crab-picking house in the summer starting in 1876. Today it houses a nice seafood deli and a top-notch museum commemorating the Chesapeake's fisherman and the Eastport neighborhood of Annapolis.

STEAMBOAT WHARF OYSTERS ROCKEFELLER

Brandy is an alcoholic beverage distilled from fermented fruit juices. In addition to its attractiveness as a beverage, brandy has its uses in cooking. Applejack brandy is delicious whether drunk from a glass or consumed in a recipe—it is, of course, made from distilled apple juice.

TOMATO/GARLIC OIL
- 5–6 cloves garlic, smashed
- 3 tomatoes, roughly chopped
- 1 pint peanut oil

OYSTERS
- 4 tablespoons butter
- 5 shallots, sliced thin
- 3 jiggers applejack
- 24 oysters in shells
- 1 cup heavy cream
  salt and pepper

- 1 bunch arugula, cleaned and cut in 1-inch chiffonade
  rock salt
  grated Parmigiano-Reggiano cheese
  chopped chives

Tomato/Garlic Oil: In a medium saucepan, sauté tomatoes in 1 tablespoon of oil and add garlic. Sauté for 1 minute, add the remaining oil, and simmer 20 minutes to infuse flavors.

Oysters: Shuck the oysters, discarding the liquor and top shells and retaining the deep bottom shells. In a large sauté pan, heat butter and brown it slightly over medium heat. Add the shallots and cook until they sweat. Deglaze with the applejack, reduce, and then add cream, salt, and pepper. Add the oysters and cook until they are plump and curling. Remove the oysters and set aside. Reduce the sauce to thicken.

In another large sauté pan, add 1 tablespoon of the Tomato/Garlic Oil and when hot, quickly toss the arugula and cook until wilted. Cover a baking sheet with rock salt and place the oyster shells on the salt. Make layers in each shell as follows: arugula on the bottom, then an oyster, then Parmigiano-Reggiano cheese. Put under the broiler until the cheese is golden. Garnish with chopped chives.

Serves 6.

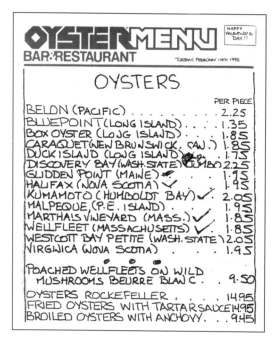

*W*hen my friend Bryan Hatchett, the famous New York photographer, visited the Grand Central Oyster Bar and Restaurant, he brought back a copy of the menu, but he neglected to bring any oysters. Thanks anyway, Bryan!

OYSTER CATCHERS OYSTERS ROCKEFELLER

 The alliance of oysters with sour cream and whipped cream would have King Neptune singing one of my favorite oyster tunes, "I Want to Get Inside Your Shell and Slurp Until I'm Well." Wasn't that covered by the Mannheim Steamroller back in '79?

24	**oysters in shells**
1½	**cups sour cream, divided**
5	**cloves garlic, chopped, divided**
2	**cups chopped raw spinach**
	salt and freshly ground black pepper
6	**tablespoons grated Parmigiano-Reggiano cheese**
	breadcrumbs
2	**tablespoons butter**
1	**cup homemade whipping cream**

Shuck and drain the oysters, discarding the oyster liquor and top shells and retaining the deep shells.

Mix ¼ cup of the sour cream with a little chopped garlic, salt, and pepper, put a teaspoon of the mixture in each oyster shell, and cover with an oyster. In a bowl, mix the spinach with the rest of the sour cream, the rest of the garlic, and salt and pepper to taste.

Top each oyster with spinach mixture and sprinkle with cheese and breadcrumbs. Dot with butter and brown under the broiler. Remove, top each oyster with a tablespoon of whipped cream, and brown again. Serve hot!

Serves 6.

"There are three kinds of oyster-eaters: those loose-minded sports who will eat anything, hot, cold, thin, thick, dead or alive, as long as it is oyster; those who will eat them raw and only raw; and those who with equal severity will eat them cooked and no way other. The first group may perhaps have the most fun, although there is a white fire about the others' bigotry that can never warm the broadminded." —M.F.K. FISHER, "CONSIDER THE OYSTER," 1941

CULLING ON BOARD OYSTERS ROCKEFELLER

This dish is quick and easy and oh, so good. The cayenne pepper will add a touch of sass, making these oysters the perfect accompaniments to a frosty, imported beer.

24	**oysters in shells**
	rock salt
1½	**sticks butter, softened**
1	**tablespoon onion juice**
¼	**cup chopped fresh parsley**
1	**teaspoon salt**
	dash of cayenne pepper
1	**cup puréed fresh spinach**
½	**cup breadcrumbs**
4	**strips cooked bacon, crumbled**

Shuck the oysters, discarding the liquor and top shells and retaining the bottom shells. Line a shallow baking pan with rock salt, place the oyster shells on the salt, and place an oyster on each shell.

Cream the butter, onion juice, and parsley. Add the salt, cayenne pepper, spinach and breadcrumbs. Spoon this mixture over the oysters and sprinkle with crumbled bacon. Broil until the edges of the oysters curl, about 5 minutes.

Serves 6.

There's something about the language of oysters that excites lyrical comment, as seen in this poem by Folger McKenzie. It makes me cry out: "Heave-ho! Bring me my dinner—and a frosty mug of beer!"

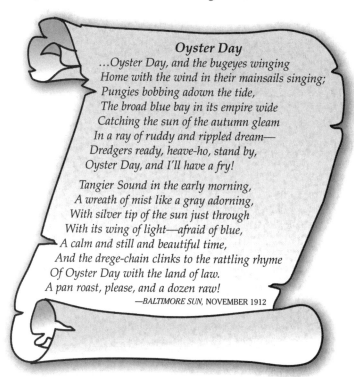

Oyster Day

*...Oyster Day, and the bugeyes winging
Home with the wind in their mainsails singing;
Pungies bobbing adown the tide,
The broad blue bay in its empire wide
Catching the sun of the autumn gleam
In a ray of ruddy and rippled dream—
Dredgers ready, heave-ho, stand by,
Oyster Day, and I'll have a fry!*

*Tangier Sound in the early morning,
A wreath of mist like a gray adorning,
With silver tip of the sun just through
With its wing of light—afraid of blue,
A calm and still and beautiful time,
And the drege-chain clinks to the rattling rhyme
Of Oyster Day with the land of law.
A pan roast, please, and a dozen raw!*

—BALTIMORE SUN, NOVEMBER 1912

CHAPTER 9
Oystering on the Chesapeake Bay
(Legend and Lore and Old Recipes)

DEBBIE PAYNE'S LUNCH BOX OYSTERS

 *Hoisin sauce is also called Peking sauce. This thick, reddish-brown sauce is sweet and spicy and is widely used in Chinese cooking. It is used as a table condiment and as a flavoring agent during meal preparation. When your guests taste these hoisin-infused oysters and ask how come they're so delicious, you can say, "Ancient Chinese secret."*

24	oysters in shells
½	cup hoisin sauce
2	tablespoons white cooking sherry
½	teaspoon garlic powder
½	teaspoon lemon pepper
½	cup freshly grated cheddar cheese

Shuck the oysters, discarding the oyster liquor and top shells and reserving the deep bottom shells. Place shells in a baking pan and place an oyster in each shell.

Mix hoisin sauce, sherry, garlic powder, and lemon pepper, and place some on each oyster. Top with grated cheese. Bake at 400°F until cheese melts.

Serves 6 as a main dish.

*P*atent tongs frame a crab shanty at Deal Island, Maryland. These tongs are raised using a foot pedal and the worker guides the oysters over the culling board, releases his catch and sends the tongs back overboard before culling (sorting out) the oysters.

HERRING BAY BAKED OYSTERS

I created this recipe for one of my ex-wives. She got the new car and the house on the water; I got the '82 Toyota, a sleeping bag and this recipe. You tell me who made out.

½ **cup butter**
½ **cup olive oil**
4 **cups breadcrumbs**
9 **garlic cloves, minced**
1 **teaspoon dried rosemary**
1 **teaspoon dried oregano**
1 **teaspoon dried basil**
   cup freshly grated Parmigiano-Reggiano cheese
1 **pint oysters and liquor**

In a large skillet, melt the butter with the olive oil over medium heat. Add the breadcrumbs and stir until they are well coated and lightly browned. Add the garlic, rosemary, oregano, basil, and cheese, and cook for 1 minute. Spread the breadcrumb mixture half an inch thick in a 9-inch cake pan or baking dish (you should have some left over). Arrange the oysters on top and cover with the remaining crumb mixture. Bake for 20 minutes and serve immediately.

Serves 4.

*S*ome *watermen unload their wares at Solomons Island, Maryland, in 1960.*

Photograph by Marion E. Warren.

OYSTERS TETRAZZINI

 A tall glass of Spanish sherry taken right from the refrigerator (preferably the crisper) goes perfectly with this rich, creamy, cheesy dish. My sister Peanutts is a lover of pasta, oysters and Spanish sherry-in whatever order.

1   **quart oysters and liquor**
4   **cups noodles (½ pound)**
    butter for greasing baking dish
    salt and pepper

SAUCE
½   **stick butter**
½   **cup all-purpose flour**
2   **teaspoons salt**
1   **teaspoon white pepper**
1   **teaspoon paprika**
2   **teaspoons Worcestershire sauce**
2½ **cups milk**
½   **cup sherry**
½   **cup Romano cheese**

TOPPING
½   **stick butter**
1   **cup breadcrumbs**
1   **cup grated Romano cheese**

Drain oysters and reserve ½ cup liquor. Cook noodles and place in a buttered baking dish.

Sauce: In a small saucepan over medium heat, melt the butter, add the flour, and stir until smooth. Add the salt, pepper, paprika, Worcestershire sauce, milk, sherry, and oyster liquor and stir until mixture is thickened. Add the cheese and stir until melted. Pour sauce over noodles.

Topping: Place the oysters on top of the noodles and sprinkle with salt and pepper. Dot with butter, sprinkle with breadcrumbs and Romano cheese, and bake 15 minutes at 400°F.

Serves 8.

*O*yster tongers, Chester River, 1986.

Photograph by Marion E. Warren.

MINCED OYSTERS

If you like dishes like Clams Casino and oyster stuffing, you'll love these baked delicacies. I suggest you eat them with the accompaniment of a good, dry champagne.

3	**pints oysters and liquor**
1½	**boxes of soda crackers**
2	**small onions**
	juice of 1½ lemons
¼	**teaspoons paprika**
1	**tablespoon Worcestershire sauce**
10	**tablespoons butter, melted**
	salt
24	**cleaned oyster shells**

Scald the oysters in their liquor, drain and chop. Reserve the liquor. Roll the crackers, but not too fine, and set them aside. Finely chop the onions fine and add the lemon juice, paprika, Worcestershire sauce, 2 tablespoons of the melted butter, and salt to taste. Add the oysters, all but ¼ cup of the cracker crumbs, and the reserved oyster liquor. The mixture should not be too soft.

Fill the shells with the oyster mixture and dust the tops lightly with the reserved ¼ cup of cracker crumbs. Drizzle each with a tablespoon of melted butter. Bake at 350°F for 8 to 10 minutes, or until heated through, and then place under the broiler until slightly browned.

Serves 10.

P̲utting them back? Here, oyster shells are being deposited back into the Bay, where they'll serve to build up oyster reefs to help the oyster population rebound. In the old days, oyster shells were used for many land-based projects: making fertilizer, constructing roads, making mortar and plaster and the like. The state of Maryland eventually saw the light, though, and began to require that the shells be returned to the Bay.

Photograph by Marion E. Warren.

Scalloped Oysters à la Frances

 Here's a great scalloped oyster dish featuring one of my favorite herbs, chervil. If you can't find chervil at your local market, I suggest you get some chervil plants, which are widely available at good nurseries and not hard to maintain. You'll be glad you did. Their mild licorice flavor is also a great compliment to eggs.

24	**oysters in shells**
1	**stick unsalted butter**
1	**garlic clove**
1	**cup fresh breadcrumbs**
2	**tablespoons finely chopped fresh parsley**
1	**tablespoon finely chopped fresh dill**
1	**tablespoon finely chopped fresh chervil**
1	**tablespoon finely chopped fresh basil**
	salt and freshly ground black pepper
¼	**cup heavy cream**
	lemon wedges

Shuck the oysters and pat them dry. Strain and reserve ¼ cup of the liquor.

In a saucepan, melt 4 tablespoons of the butter, sauté the garlic in it until tender, and discard the garlic. Stir in the breadcrumbs and parsley.

Blend the remaining butter with the dill, chervil, and basil, or process the butter and herbs in a food processor. Add a dash of salt and pepper.

Sprinkle half the breadcrumb mixture in a gratin dish or a 9-by-9-inch casserole. Arrange the oysters on top in a single layer, drizzle with the oyster liquor, and dot with the herb butter. Cover with the remaining crumbs and drizzle with the cream.

Bake at 375°F for 15 minutes or until the top is golden brown and bubbling. Serve with lemon wedges.

Serves 4.

The Mariners' Museum, Newport News, VA. Photograph by A. Aubrey Bodine.

In honor of these watermen, I offer the following verse from William Shakespeare:

*"The man had sure a palate covered o'er
With brass or steel, that on the rocky shore
First broke the oozy oyster's pearly coat,
And risqued the living morsel down
his throat."*

DENNY'S BAKED OYSTERS

 The irresistible flavor of garlic and onion, along with seasoned crouton crumbs, makes this dish extra special. It's like life in Bay country: rich, varied and extremely fragrant. As I say, garlic shared is the best perfume.

24	**oysters in shells**
1	**stick butter**
1	**small onion or 3 green onions, coarsely chopped**
6	**garlic cloves, coarsely chopped**
½	**teaspoon Italian seasoning**
½	**teaspoon lemon pepper**
8	**drops Tabasco sauce**
½	**teaspoon Worcestershire sauce**
½	**teaspoon salt**
½	**lemon**
1	**cup seasoned crouton crumbs**
	Parmigiano-Reggiano cheese
	crackers

Shuck the oysters and discard the shells and oyster liquor.

Melt the butter and pour it into a small baking dish or glass pie plate. Add the onions, garlic, Italian seasoning, lemon pepper, Tabasco sauce, Worcestershire, and salt.

Place the oysters on top in one layer, if possible. Squeeze lemon over the oysters. Cover with crouton crumbs and sprinkle lightly with Parmigiano-Reggiano cheese. Bake at 350°F for ½ hour or until golden brown. Serve with crackers.

Serves 4.

The Mariners' Museum, Newport News, VA. Photograph by A. Aubrey Bodine.

*F*olks up in Baltimore have to go somewhere to unwind on the weekends. But out here on the Shore, all we gotta do is look around to unwind— there's nothing more peaceful.

SISTER JUDY'S OYSTER PUDDING

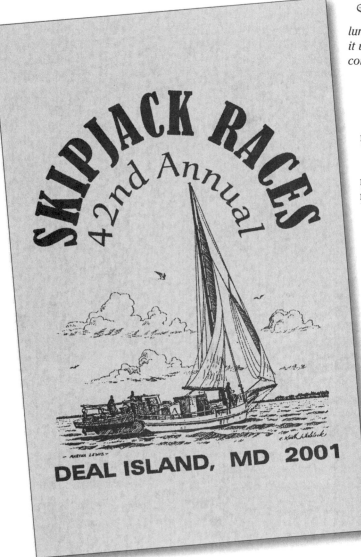

This delightful dish is light and creamy and can be served as a brunch dish, lunch dish, supper dish, or any ol' time dish. Serve it with a salad and fresh fruit and you have a complete meal.

6	slices buttered bread, cubed
4	ounces sharp cheddar cheese, grated
1	pint oysters and liquor
2	eggs
¼	cup minced green onion
2	tablespoons minced white onion
1	teaspoon salt
¼	teaspoon black pepper
⅛	teaspoon Tabasco sauce
3	cups milk
	butter

Butter a 2-quart casserole dish. Place half the bread cubes in the disk and add the grated cheddar cheese. Drain the oysters, discarding liquor, add them to the dish, and top with the remaining bread cubes.

In a bowl, beat the eggs, green onions, white onions, salt, pepper, Tabasco sauce, and milk. Pour this mixture over the casserole and dot with butter. Bake at 325°F for 1¼ hours.

Serves 6.

One of the special events that make the Chesapeake the Chesapeake is the annual skipjack racing at Deal Island, Maryland. When they're not racing, these skipjacks still dredge ("drudge") for oysters under the power of enormous sails. Piloting one of these traditional craft isn't easy. To quote skipjack captain Stanford White: "I watched the good captains and they learned me."

POACHED OYSTERS ON TOAST

Poaching oysters simply means to cook them gently in liquid heated just below the boiling point. When the liquid's surface begins to quiver from the heat, the water's ready for poaching.

4   strips lean bacon (breakfast style)
1   pint oysters with liquor
    juice of 1 lemon
6   slices crisp toast

In a skillet, fry the bacon until crisp. Remove, leaving about 2 teaspoons bacon fat in skillet, and drain on paper towels.

Add the oysters and liquor to the skillet and cook over medium heat until the edges begin to curl. Mix the lemon juice with the oysters.

Serve on toast with bacon crumbled over each serving.

Serves 6.

Stanford White was not only a good skipjack captain, he knew just how to market his boat, the F.C. Lewis.

Chesapeake   Bay   Skipjack
F. C. LEWIS
Size 39.0 x 14.6 x 3.0 feet
Built 1907 at Hopkins, Virginia
Captain   -   Stanford   White
Home port - Wenona, Maryland
In 1982 she had won 8 out of 23 yearly races.

195

BACON-BAKED OYSTERS

 "Obviously, if you don't love life you can't enjoy an oyster."

—ELEANOR CLARK, "THE OYSTERS OF LOCMARIAQUER"

(I would say that the words "oyster" and "bacon" could be used interchangeably in that astute observation.)

24	oysters in shells
6	slices bacon, each cut into 4 pieces
1	cup crumbs from round, buttery crackers
½	cup mayonnaise
2	tablespoons chopped chives
1	teaspoon lemon juice
1	teaspoon Tabasco sauce
½	teaspoon Dijon mustard
2	pounds rock salt
¼	cup grated Parmigiano-Reggiano cheese

Shuck oysters and reserve the deep shells; place the oysters in a colander to drain.

Cook the bacon until limp, but not brown; drain and set aside.

Combine the cracker crumbs, mayonnaise, chives, lemon juice, and mustard. Mix well and set aside.

Sprinkle rock salt in a 15-by-10-by-1-inch baking sheet. Arrange the oyster shells on the salt and place an oyster in each shell. Spread the crumb mixture over each oyster, top with a piece of bacon, and sprinkle with cheese. Bake at 400°F for 8 to 10 minutes or until the bacon is crisp.

Serves 4 to 6.

"Turkle" North proudly shows us what a freshly shucked oyster looks like. Turkle was a waterman most of his life. Today, he's a volunteer at the Chesapeake Bay Maritime Museum in St. Michaels, Maryland. (Thanks, Turkle. It was delicious.)

OYSTERS ON A BED OF SPINACH

This is a winning recipe from a Chesapeake Appreciation Days Oyster Cooking Contest held long ago. I've used it a number of times over the last 20 years. Credit goes to Arceli C. Suley of Silver Spring, Maryland.

½ **cup rice vinegar**
¼ **cup chopped green onions**
4 **cloves garlic, minced**
1 **tablespoon sherry**
1 **teaspoon salt**
½ **teaspoon freshly ground black pepper**
1½ **pints oysters and liquor**
¾ **pound fresh spinach**
3 **tablespoons cooking oil**

Make a marinade by mixing the rice vinegar, green onions, garlic, sherry, salt, and pepper. Marinate the oysters for 1 hour. Steam them in the marinade for 5 minutes and set aside. Wash the spinach and cut each leaf in half. Heat the cooking oil in a skillet and stir-fry the spinach for 1 minute. Spread the spinach on a serving dish and place the oysters on top. Serve over hot cooked rice.

Serves 4.

*H*ayes, *Virginia, watermen Thomas Brown, left, and Ernest West Jr. tong for oysters in the James River.*

Photograph by Bryan Hatchett.

OYSTERS AU GRATIN

Photograph by Vince Lupo.

I look for recipes that are imaginative, easy to prepare and, above all, that taste good. Just be careful with the cayenne pepper in this recipe—a little goes a long way.

1	pint oysters in liquor
1	cup water
1	tablespoon butter
2	tablespoons all-purpose flour
½	cup milk
	salt
	cayenne pepper
	grated Parmigiano-Reggiano cheese

Drain the oysters, reserving the oyster liquor. In a saucepan, scald the oysters in 1 cup water, drain, and set aside. In saucepan, melt the butter, mix in the flour, and stir until smooth. Add the milk and ½ cup of the oyster liquor. Stir gently and season to taste with salt and cayenne pepper.

Cut the oysters into quarters and stir gently into the sauce. Allow the mixture to boil for 3 minutes. Put in a deep dish, sprinkle liberally with Parmigiano-Reggiano cheese, and bake at 400°F for 12 minutes, or until golden brown.

Serves 4.

Here we see a picture of the oysterman's tools. Even standing still, and in a photograph, they make my back hurt! Here's a hearty thanks to all the men who work their butts off to get us the oysters we love so much.

TANGIER ISLAND OYSTERS AND SPAGHETTI

Don't be intimidated by the thought of making a bechamel sauce, which is simply a milk-based white sauce thickened with roux (flour and fat in equal proportions). Bechamel sauce is considered a great "mother sauce," because so many other sauces can be made from it by adding different herbs, cheeses and other ingredients. Note: If you like a thinner sauce, just add a little more milk.

8   **ounces spaghetti broken into 1-inch pieces**
4   **tablespoons butter, divided**
1   **pint oysters and liquor**
    salt and freshly ground black pepper
½   **cup fine breadcrumbs**

BECHAMEL SAUCE
3   **cups milk**
⅓   **cup butter**
2   **tablespoons grated onion**
⅓   **cup all-purpose flour**
2   **sprigs fresh parsley**
6   **black peppercorns**
    pinch of freshly grated nutmeg
    salt

Cook the spaghetti in boiling salted water until tender. Drain and blanch.

Use 2 tablespoons of the butter to grease 4 ramekins; line the bottoms with the spaghetti.

In a saucepan, heat the oysters in their liquor until the edges curl. Drain. Place half the oysters on top of the spaghetti in each ramekin and sprinkle with salt and pepper to taste. Add half the bechamel sauce (instructions below). Add another layer of oysters and another of bechamel sauce.

Melt the other 2 tablespoons of butter and mix with the breadcrumbs. Sprinkle this mixture on top of the oysters. Bake 20 minutes at 400°F until mixture is heated thoroughly and crumbs are golden brown.

Serves 4.

Bechamel sauce: In a saucepan, warm the milk over very low heat. Meanwhile, melt the butter in another saucepan and add onion. Sauté the onion until golden; do not allow to turn brown. Stir in the flour and cook over low heat for 3 minutes or until bubbly. Gradually add milk, whisking constantly.

Cook until the sauce thickens; add parsley, peppercorns, nutmeg, and salt. Keep heat very low and continue cooking for 20 to 25 minutes, uncovered, stirring frequently. Thin with a little milk, if desired. Strain through a fine sieve.

Makes about 3 cups. (Note: If made in advance, float 1 tablespoon melted butter on top. To serve, reheat in top of double boiler over simmering water; beat in butter.)

*T*his is a sight that skipjack captains love to see: a great haul of oysters, freshly pulled from the Chesapeake and ready for market.

The Mariners' Museum, Newport News, VA.

Photograph by A. Aubrey Bodine.

TILGHMAN ISLAND OYSTER BAKE

On Tilghman Island, Maryland, it is believed that the women are so beautiful because of all the oysters they eat. In China, it is believed that oysters "cure" freckles. Are these two notions related? I doubt it, because I'm kind of a freckles man, myself.

3	slices bacon
3	tablespoons chopped onion
2	tablespoons chopped green pepper
1	stalk celery, diced
1	teaspoon lemon juice
½	teaspoon pepper
½	teaspoon Worcestershire sauce
1	dash Tabasco sauce
1	pint oysters and liquor
	butter for greasing baking dish

Chop bacon and fry until brown. Drain on paper towels. In the hot fat, fry the onion, pepper, and celery until tender, Add the lemon juice, pepper, Worcestershire sauce, and Tabasco sauce, and mix well.

Drain the oysters and discard the liquor. Grease a baking dish, arrange the oysters in it, and spread the onion/pepper/celery mixture on top. Crumble bacon over the top and bake at 350°F for 8 to 10 minutes.

Serves 4.

Sailing into her third century, Rebecca T. Ruark is the oldest example of Maryland's state boat symbol, the skipjack. In the late 1890s, hundreds of skipjacks plied the Chesapeake Bay to dredge for oysters. Today, only a dozen working boats remain. Now, 115 years since Rebecca's planks were cut, she carries passengers to bring alive maritime history and the waterman's culture and to describe the present-day ecology of the Bay. Captain "Wadey" Murphy's knowledge, humor, and Tilghman Island charm make him a well-informed historian of and a wonderful commentator of Chesapeake Bay life. Call 410-829-3976 for your cruise schedule.

OLD TRADITION STEAMED OYSTERS

Oysters with vinegar and crackers are a long-established tradition among my friendly circles. Give this combination a try and tell me you don't have some friendly thoughts afterwards.

24	oysters in shells
½	cup apple cider vinegar
½	teaspoon seafood seasoning
½	teaspoon pepper
½	teaspoon salt
	oyster crackers

Place the oysters in a steaming basket over an inch of boiling; do not submerge. Steam them until they barely begin to pop open. Finish opening them with a shucking knife. In a small bowl stir together the vinegar, seafood seasoning, salt, and pepper. Dip the steamed oysters in this mixture and serve with oyster crackers.

Serves 4.

Ol' skipjack Number 29, the Rebecca T. Ruark, *was built on Taylors Island, just southwest of Cambridge, Maryland, before the turn of the last century. Today she's owned by skipjack captain par excellence Wade Murphy. (Note: The old tradition called for naming the first boat after the man of the house and the second one after his wife. Well, they say women usually outlive their husbands. Mr. Ruark, may you rest in peace, wherever you are.)*

SHERRIED OYSTERS

Take note that sherries range from exquisite to blah-blah-blah. Don't cook with any sherry that you wouldn't drink. Unless it's someone named Sherry. In that case, please, cook away.

1	**pint oysters and liquor**
1	**cup water**
	salt
¼	**cup sherry**
	cayenne pepper
¼	**cup heavy cream**
2	**egg yolks**
	toast
	fresh parsley

Drain the oysters and discard the oyster liquor. In a small saucepan, boil oysters, water, and a pinch of salt for 5 minutes. Drain. Return the oysters to the empty saucepan and pour the sherry over them. Season to taste with salt and cayenne pepper and cook for 3 minutes.

Add the cream and cook 6 minutes longer. Place the egg yolks in a cup and stir in 2 tablespoons of the hot sherry mixture. Return the egg yolk/sherry mixture to the pan and simmer for 3 minutes, stirring gently. Serve on toast and garnish with parsley.

Serves 4.

*B*uy *boats, generally not active on the Bay anymore, used to sidle up to skipjacks while the skipjacks were still out on the water on extended fishing trips. The buy boat captains would buy oysters straight off the skipjacks and take them to market—then the skipjacks could stay out and catch more oysters.*

CHESTER RIVER SEAFOOD MEDLEY

This seafood medley can be served as a side dish or alongside crabcakes and roasted or grilled meats. You can also throw in a lobster tail, a favorite touch of mine when I'm looking to impress.

2   **cups butter, divided**
1   **tablespoon all-purpose flour**
2   **cups milk**
1   **pint oysters and liquor**
½   **pound fresh crabmeat**
½   **pound cooked shrimp, peeled**
    salt and pepper
    dash of Tabasco sauce
½   **cup sherry**

In a double boiler, melt 1 tablespoon of the butter. Mix in the flour and stir until smooth. Add the milk, salt and pepper to taste, and Tabasco sauce, and stir until the mixture is thick. Remove from heat.

In a large saucepan, melt the rest of the butter and allow to reach boiling point. Drain the oysters, discard liquor, and add oysters, crabmeat, and shrimp to the butter and sauté for 5 minutes. Add the sauce and sherry and mix thoroughly.

Serves 6.

On the deck of this stilted house is a woman with a rifle and a good eye. She has one of the most unusual jobs in Tidewater Virginia: She is an oyster watcher and keeps poachers away from valuable—and privately leased—oyster beds. Here, she watches over Toms Cove, near Chincoteague, Virginia, one of the best oyster grounds in America.

Photograph by A. Aubrey Bodine, © 2003 Jennifer B. Bodine, courtesy of AAubreyBodine.com.

203

PACKING HOUSE OYSTERS NEWPORT NEWS

 This recipe produces some of the most tender seafood you've ever eaten—and some of the tastiest, too.

2   **tablespoons butter**
8   **button mushrooms, quartered**
1   **teaspoon seafood seasoning**
2   **tablespoons freshly chopped garlic**
1   **pint oysters and liquor**
1   **ear corn, blanched and scraped**
⅔   **cup fresh string beans, blanched**
2   **tablespoons diced pimento**
½   **cup seafood stock**
8   **ounces fresh linguine, any style**
2   **tablespoons roux**
2   **tablespoons chopped fresh parsley**
3   **tablespoons chopped scallions**
4   **ounces lump crabmeat**

In a large saucepan, melt butter and sauté mushrooms, seafood seasoning, and garlic over medium-high heat for 2 minutes. Drain oysters and add along with corn, string beans, and pimento. Sauté for 2 minutes. Add stock and linguine and bring to a slight simmer. Fold in roux until the sauce thickens, then reduce heat. Fold in parsley, scallions, and crabmeat and bring up to heat. Serve immediately.

Serves 4.

*B*ridge of Boats: When this tonging fleet—which sails out of the towns of Deep Creek and Menchville, Virginia—is anchored in Deep Creek, it literally forms a bridge of boats between the two towns. At times, there are a thousand boats riding at anchor. The fleet tongs for seed oysters on the James River.

Photograph by A. Aubrey Bodine. Courtesy of the Mariners' Museum, Newport News, VA.

OYSTERS MAGPIE

This dish is great served over rice, with Dutch noodles or plenty of mashed pota-toes. This is not a quickie recipe, but I think you'll find that it's more than worth the effort.

1   **quart oysters and liquor**
2   **small frying chickens, cut up**
1   **cup olive oil**
1   **cup dry white wine**
1   **tablespoons dried oregano**
2   **tablespoons dried rosemary**
1   **teaspoon dried sweet basil**
1   **garlic clove, chopped**
1   **large can (about 30 ounces)**
    Italian tomatoes
1   **green pepper, sliced**
½   **cup chopped fresh parsley**

1½   **pound shelled raw shrimp**
1   **tablespoon fresh mint, chopped**
    cooked rice

Drain the oysters, reserving the liquor.

In a large skillet, sauté the chicken in the olive oil over high heat, turning often to sear and browning the outside. When the chicken is brown, add the wine, oyster liquor, oregano, rosemary, basil, and garlic; lower heat and cook for 5 minutes. Add the tomatoes, green pepper, and parsley, and boil, stirring occasionally, for 30 minutes or until the pepper is tender. Add the shrimp, oysters, and mint; cook 15 minutes more. Serve over rice.

Serves 8.

The dredge—versus the less-invasive tong— was introduced on the Chesapeake Bay in the early 1800s, but it wasn't until after the Civil War that dredges were made legal in Maryland waters. There is no way I could have been a waterman back when they hand-cranked these babies —unless I was guaranteed a bushel or two of the profits afterwards.

Photograph by A. Aubrey Bodine, © 2003 Jennifer B. Bodine, courtesy of AAubreyBodine.com.

TwoJohns Choptank Oysters

This delicious dish is like many served around Bay country in that it's important to taste the sauce and correct the seasonings before adding the mushroom caps. Otherwise, you might over-season, as the mushrooms will shrink down and concentrate the flavors.

1   pint oysters and liquor
½   teaspoon lemon juice
1   tablespoons butter
1   can (8–10 ounces) cream of mushroom
        soup
½   teaspoon Worcestershire sauce
1   cup milk
½   cup chopped onions
2   cups cracker crumbs
12   large fresh mushroom caps
        paprika

In a saucepan, simmer the oysters in their liquor with lemon juice and butter until their edges curl. Drain the oysters, reserving the liquor, and set aside.

In another saucepan, combine the cream of mushroom soup, milk, and onions and heat to a boil. Stir in the Worcestershire sauce and remove from heat.

Place 1 cup of the cracker crumbs in a well-buttered casserole and cover with half of the drained oysters, half of the mushroom soup mixture, and half the reserved oyster liquor. Repeat these layers: cracker crumbs, oysters, soup, liquor. Then arrange the mushroom caps on top and sprinkle with paprika. Bake for 30 minutes at 375°F.

Serves 4.

Photograph by A. Aubrey Bodine, © 2003 Jennifer B. Bodine, courtesy of AAubreyBodine.com.

"Mountain of Oyster Shells": This A. Aubrey Bodine photo, taken circa 1950, shows shell piles outside an oyster-packing plant on the shores of Hampton Creek near Hampton, Virginia.

OLD MANOR HOUSE OYSTER DELIGHT

Blue cheese, sour cream and hard-boiled eggs may seem like an unusual combination when partnered with oysters—but trust me: It's fantastic! I first encountered this dish at a Thanksgiving buffet back in 1985 and have been preparing it with regularity since then.

6	**ounces blue cheese**
6	**tablespoons butter**
6	**tablespoons finely chopped celery**
1	**tablespoon Worcestershire sauce**
½	**cup sour cream**
1	**quart oysters**
½	**lemon**
2	**hard-boiled eggs, chopped fine**
	paprika

In the top of a double boiler over simmering water, melt the cheese and butter. Add the chopped celery and cook for about 5 minutes. Add the Worcestershire sauce and sour cream. Divide the oysters among 6 individual baking dishes and sprinkle them with lemon juice. Stir the chopped eggs into the cheese sauce and pour the sauce over the oysters. Bake for about 10 minutes at 375°F and serve piping hot sprinkled with paprika.

Serves 6

Another beautiful shot by A. Aubrey Bodine shows "Choptank Oyster Dredgers" in 1948. Bodine took this picture while on assignment for the Sun *magazine. The large skipjack is the* Maggie Lee; *the small one on the horizon is the* Lucy Tyler.

Photograph by A. Aubrey Bodine, © 2003 Jennifer B. Bodine, courtesy of AAubreyBodine.com.

Hampton Roads Oysters Bryan

Health-conscious cooks and gardeners alike have long enjoyed the many benefits of herbs grown in the kitchen garden. The dried renditions can easily be made by hanging most herbs stem-side-up and just letting them air dry.

½   **cup fine, dry breadcrumbs**
½   **cup grated Parmigiano-Reggiano cheese**
2   **teaspoons dried basil**
2   **teaspoons minced fresh parsley**
1   **teaspoon dried oregano**
½   **teaspoon salt**
½   **teaspoon pepper**
½   **teaspoon garlic powder**
1   **pint oysters and liquor**
2   **tablespoons olive oil**
2   **tablespoons dry white wine**
2   **tablespoons fresh lemon juice**

Butter a 9-inch baking dish. Combine breadcrumbs, cheese, basil, parsley, oregano, salt, pepper, and garlic powder. Put about ⅓ of the crum mixture into the baking dish. Drain the oysters, discarding liquor, and place them in a single layer on top of the crumbs. Top with the remaining crumbs. Mix together the olive oil, wine, and lemon juice and sprinkle over the top. Bake uncovered at 425°F for10 to 12 minutes, or until the oysters are set and the crumbs are browned.

Serves 4.

The dredge is essentially a broad iron scoop two to six feet wide, with a toothed edge to dig into the oyster reefs and a chain bag to hold the oysters. Back in their day, dredges had to be winched up by hand, as seen in this photo. Fellahs? How about a beer?

CHAPTER 10
The Opulent Oyster
(Oyster Entrées)

Garlic Oysters à la Briggs White

*As my old friend Briggs explained to me:
When Columbus sailed from Spain looking for the East Indies, nutmeg was one of the
spices for which he was searching. So when I was
searching for a spice to bring this dish to excellence, nutmeg was my choice, too.*

1   **stick butter, softened**
5   **cloves garlic, minced**
¼   **cup chopped fresh parsley**
2   **shallots, minced**
    salt
1   **teaspoon freshly ground black pepper**

    freshly grated nutmeg
2   **teaspoons cognac**
2   **teaspoons dry white wine**
24 **oysters in shells**
    rock salt

In a mixing bowl, beat together the butter,
garlic, parsley, shallots, salt, pepper, nutmeg,
cognac, and wine. Cover and refrigerate
overnight.

Shuck the oysters, leaving them in their
deep shells and discarding the top shells and
liquor. Line a baking pan with rock salt and set
the oysters on top. Top each oyster with 2 teaspoons of the butter mixture. Bake until the
edges of the oysters curl and the butter is bubbly, about 10 minutes. Serve hot.

Serves 4.

Photograph by Ron White.

*Here's Briggs in the Crab Lab test kitchen with
another dish hot from the oven. Briggs, open
another beer, will ya?*

WYE ISLAND OYSTER BAKE

Bell peppers are so named because of their rather bell-like shape. They have a mild, sweet flavor and crisp, exceedingly juicy flesh. When young, the majority of bell peppers are a bright green, but there are also yellow, orange, purple, brown, and red bell peppers. The red bells are simply vine-ripened green bells. Because they've ripened longer, they're very sweet.

- 1 **pint oysters and liquor**
- 2 **large red bell peppers**
- ½ **cup crushed saltine crackers**
- 4 **tablespoons melted butter**
  salt and freshly ground black pepper
- 2 **tablespoons minced fresh parsley**

Drain the oysters and reserve the liquor. Cut the tops off the peppers and scoop out the seeds. Parboil them by placing them in a saucepan, covering them with water, and boiling for 7 minutes.

In a mixing bowl, combine the cracker crumbs and melted butter. Place a thick layer of buttered crumbs in the bottom of each pepper. Place 3 oysters in each pepper. Season with salt and pepper and drizzle with reserved oyster liquor. Top with more oysters, more crumbs, and more liquor. Repeat twice. Sprinkle with parsley and bake for 20 minutes at 375°F, or until peppers are tender and crumbs are golden brown. Serve hot.

Serves 2.

This inviting table of freshly shucked oysters was set—and subsequently ravaged—at Harrison's Chesapeake House on Maryland's Tilghman Island. Harrison's not only has great food, but its walls are covered with local memorabilia, making this Eastern Shore restaurant a sort of eat-in museum.

Photograph by Vince Lupo.

211

QUEENSTOWN OYSTER SOUFFLÉ

This dish is light and delicate. Like most soufflés, this one will fall pretty quickly after you remove it from the oven. That's okay, though. Just move fast, dammit!

1   **pint oysters and liquor**
3   **tablespoons butter**
3   **tablespoons all-purpose flour**
1   **cup milk**
1   **teaspoon salt**
⅛   **teaspoon white pepper**
     dash of ground nutmeg
3   **eggs, separated**

Drain and chop the oysters and discard the oyster liquor. In a saucepan over medium heat, melt the butter and add the flour. Add the milk and bring to a boil, stirring constantly. Cook for 3 minutes. Add the oysters, salt, pepper, nutmeg, and beaten egg yolks.

Beat the egg whites until stiff but not dry. Fold them into the oyster mixture. Pour into a buttered casserole dish and bake at 350°F for 30 minutes or until brown.

Serves 4.

This storefront advertises all you need for refined living on the Eastern Shore: oysters, soft crabs, Coke, Coors and, of course, a good dash of patriotism.

TAPPAHANNOCK STUFFED MUSHROOMS

Early Greeks and Romans are thought to have been among the first to actually cultivate mushrooms, using them in a wide variety of dishes. For this recipe, I'd recommend going with some of the standard 'shrooms, either buttons or portabellos.

FILLING

3	slices bacon, minced
3	tablespoons all-purpose flour
4	cups trimmed and chopped fresh spinach
¼	cup half-and-half
	dash of Tabasco sauce
½	cup grated Parmigiano-Reggiano cheese

TOPPING

4	ounces cream cheese
3	tablespoons minced garlic
2	green onions, thinly sliced
3	tablespoons anisette

MUSHROOMS

12	large white button mushrooms
12	oysters in shells
	salt and pepper
1	tablespoon minced red bell pepper
	lemon juice

Filling: In a large saucepan over medium-high heat, sauté the bacon until crisp. Stir in the flour, followed by the spinach and half-and-half. Cook, stirring well, until thick. Stir in the Tabasco sauce. Remove from the heat, fold in the Parmigiano-Reggiano cheese, and set aside.

Topping: Soften the cream cheese at room temperature. Stir in the garlic, green onions, and anisette until creamy.

Mushrooms: Pull the stems off the mushrooms, leaving a cavity in the cap. Discard the stems. Season the caps with salt and pepper. Divide the spinach filling evenly among the mushrooms.

Shuck the oysters and discard the shells and oyster liquor. Lightly press one oyster into each spinach-filled mushroom. Top each oyster with about 1 teaspoon of the cream cheese topping, spreading it out to partially cover the oyster.

Place the mushrooms on a lightly oiled baking pan. Sprinkle each mushroom with a little minced red bell pepper. Bake at 325°F until the mushrooms are tender, the filling is hot, and oysters are just cooked, 8 to 12 minutes. As soon as you take the mushrooms from the oven, sprinkle with lemon juice.

Serves 4.

I loved this letterhead from the moment I saw it. I cropped out the company name and left the York River Oysters logo. It made for a wonderful, one-of-a-kind tee shirt.

213

GALESVILLE OYSTER STUFFING (FOR 12-POUND TURKEY)

Oyster stuffing or dressing is a savory mixture flavored with bits of oyster, sausage, onion, celery and spices. This version will make the Thanksgiving Day turkey get up and dance a quick jig before the carving.

	turkey giblets
½	**pound pork sausage**
3	**strips bacon**
½	**teaspoon salt**
½	**teaspoon pepper**
½	**teaspoon poultry seasoning**
½	**teaspoon dried thyme**
2-3	**ribs celery**
1	**medium onion**
½	**pint oysters and liquor**
	large loaf French bread
1	**tablespoon melted butter**

Precook giblets in water for 45 minutes. In a food processor, grind the giblets with the bacon until coarse. Place the sausage in a large pot and add the ground giblet mixture, salt, pepper, poultry seasoning, and thyme. Sauté for 15 minutes.

In a food processor, coarsely grind the celery and onion and add them to the sausage-giblet mixture. Cook until the vegetables are tender. Drain and chop the oysters. Add them and cook for three more minutes. Soak the bread in water for 5 minutes. Remove and squeeze out the moisture. Break the bread up and combine well with other ingredients. Drizzle melted butter on top and toss to combine.

Loosely stuff the turkey. Place the leftover stuffing in a bowl and bake it separately.

Photograph by Vince Lupo.

As our enthusiasm for collecting oyster cans and art grows, so too do prices for prime bivalve-i-cana pieces like these. Luckily, bargain hunters like me can still find great deals on these interesting collectibles, particularly in the smaller antiques shops along Route 13 on Maryland's Eastern Shore. Tell 'em Whitey sent you.

EASTON CORNBREAD & OYSTER STUFFING

Most folks rambling about the Eastern Shore find it all too easy to blow by Easton on their way to St. Michaels or Oxford, Maryland. Not necessarily a good idea. Not only does Easton possess some great historic architecture as part of a revitalized downtown, but also, you may be lucky enough to find this dish on the menu there in the fall.

- 4 tablespoons butter
- 2 large ribs celery with leaves, chopped
- 1 large yellow onion, chopped
- 1 pint oysters and liquor
- 1 package (8 ounces) cornbread stuffing mix
- 4 slices whole-wheat bread, cut into ½-inch cubes
- ½ cup chicken stock
- ½ cup chopped fresh parsley
- 1 tablespoon crumbled dried sage
- 2 teaspoons crumbled dried thyme
- 1 teaspoon crumbled dried marjoram
- ½ teaspoon salt
- ½ teaspoon black pepper

In a Dutch oven over medium heat, melt the butter. Add the celery and onions and cook, stirring occasionally, just until tender—8 to 10 minutes. Remove from the heat.

Drain and chop the oysters, reserving the oyster liquor. Add the oysters, cornbread stuffing mix, bread cubes, ½ cup of the reserved oyster liquor, the chicken stock, parsley, sage, thyme, marjoram, salt, and pepper, and toss well.

Spoon the stuffing into a lightly buttered 2- to 2½-quart baking dish. Cover tightly with foil and bake at 325°F for 45 minutes.

Serves 10.

I'm Oscar the oyster, a holiday blessing
To appetites wanting turkey with dressing.
When served on the half-shell, I help introduce
The year's biggest feast, so put me to use!

Cambridge Oyster Bake

Savory baked dishes were quite common in our family's house when I was growing up on the Western Shore. I remember after Mom popped this dish in the oven, I'd stand by the stove, and everyone would accuse me of "stealing" the heat from the stove to stay warm. Well, actually I was just waiting for a bite of oyster bake.

1	cup uncooked brown rice
2	cups boiling salted water
1	stick butter, divided
½	cup chopped shallots
½	pound fresh mushrooms, thinly sliced
1	teaspoon seasoned salt, divided
1	cup dry white wine
1	pint oysters and liquor
⅛	teaspoon freshly ground black pepper

Cook the rice in the salted water for about 25 minutes or according to package directions.

In a saucepan, melt 4 tablespoons of the butter and sauté the shallots and mushrooms. Sprinkle with half the seasoned salt; add the wine and simmer for 5 minutes.

Combine the mushroom mixture with the rice and place in a buttered 3-quart casserole dish.

Drain the oysters, discarding the oyster liquor. Melt the remaining butter. Dip each oyster in melted butter and arrange them over the rice mixture. Sprinkle with pepper and the remaining seasoned salt. Bake, uncovered, at 350°F for 30 minutes.

Serves 6.

9252. UNLOADING OYSTER LUGGERS, BALTIMORE. MD.

This 1905 postcard is titled "Unloading Oyster Luggers, Baltimore." Now, I don't know about the lugging part, but here's something I could do for a living: Like these fine men, stand around and look important.

SOUTH COUNTY SCALLOPED OYSTERS (FOR A CROWD)

Buffet-style dining is fun, whether supper is for two or twenty! I recommend inviting one or two more people than you really have room for. The closer spaces tend to get people talking, drinking, and eating.

- 8   sticks butter
- 6   quarts breadcrumbs
- 4   tablespoons salt
- 1   teaspoon paprika plus additional for sprinkling on top
- 1   teaspoon pepper
- 3   gallons oysters and liquor
     milk

In a large stockpot, melt the butter. Mix in the breadcrumbs, salt, paprika, and pepper.

Drain the oysters, straining and reserving the oyster liquor.

Spread a third of the crumb mixture in a buttered baking pan. Cover with half the oysters, another third of the crumb mixture, and the remaining oysters.

Combine the oyster liquor with enough milk to make 1 gallon. Pour this mixture over the oysters. Spread on the remaining crumbs and sprinkle with paprika. Bake at 375°F for 30 minutes.

Serves 100 (6-ounce servings).

I snapped this photo of Sherberts Farm Market a dozen years ago. Marjorie and Gordon Sherbert took great pride in their Tracey's Landing location. I know: I bought many an oyster from them. Muskrats? Never!

CHESAPEAKE BEACH OYSTERS & CREAMED CHICKEN

When I was a kid, Mom Schmidt would make a dish that was something like this except she used canned tuna. As the years passed, I started substituting oysters for the tuna and adding a little sherry. While the result is a little subtler on the palate, Mom's version is still the best I'll ever taste.

1	**stick butter**
¼	**cup all-purpose flour**
2	**cups milk**
1	**pint oysters and liquor**
3	**cups cut up cooked chickcn breast**
1	**tablespoon sherry**
1	**teaspoon salt**
¼	**teaspoon pepper**
	toast points
	parsley sprigs

In a saucepan over medium heat, melt the butter. Stir in the flour and gradually add the milk and cook, stirring constantly, until thickened.

Drain the oysters and discard the oyster liquor. Stir the oysters, chicken, sherry, salt, and pepper into the white sauce. Simmer for 10 minutes. Serve over toast points garnished with parsley sprigs.

Serves 6.

The Municipal Fish Wharf in Washington, D.C.— on the shore of the Potomac River—draws crowds of seafood lovers to its docks, which are in the shadow of the Washington Monument. After all that strolling on the Mall, how about a herring?

Photograph by Pat Piper.

218

GRASONVILLE OYSTER BAKE

No matter what season you visit Grasonville on Maryland's Kent Island, you're likely to run into fellow oyster lovers, many of whom live on the Shore and work in Washington or Annapolis. If I lived in a bedroom community, eating oysters would make even more sense than it does here in Crisfield.

1 **quart oysters and liquor**
6 **tablespoons butter**
2 **tablespoons all-purpose flour**
1 **cup cream**
4 **tablespoons sherry**
   pinch of cayenne pepper
1 **teaspoon grated lemon rind**
1 **teaspoon anchovy paste**
1 **cup breadcrumbs**
   pinch of salt
   pinch of paprika
1 **cup grated Parmigiano-Reggiano cheese**

Drain the oysters, discard the oyster liquor, and set the oysters aside.

In a saucepan over medium heat, melt the butter and stir in the flour. Slowly stir in the cream, sherry, cayenne pepper, lemon rind, and anchovy paste. Bring this sauce to a boil and then pour into a shallow buttered baking dish. Top with the oysters and sprinkle with the breadcrumbs, salt, paprika, and Parmigiano-Reggiano cheese. Bake at 400°F for 5 minutes.

Serves 8.

If I put a sign outside my place—"Oyster Donations Needed"—do you think it'll work? I'm willing to give it a try. In the name of those in need.

LEONARDTOWN OYSTER-STUFFED FLOUNDER

Nestled on the Potomac River, the picturesque waterfront hamlet of Leonardtown, Maryland, has a rich tradition of Bay Country cooking. Today, Leonardtown hosts the annual U.S. Oyster Shucking Championships each fall.

8   **pieces (3 ounces each) flounder filet**
     salt
2   **tablespoons lemon juice**
1   **cup oysters**
2   **eggs**
1   **cup plus 2 tablespoons seasoned bread-crumbs**

Sprinkle both sides of the flounder filets with salt, place in a large bowl, and sprinkle with lemon juice. Set aside to marinate.

Lay 4 of the filets on a baking pan. Beat 1 of the eggs. Place 1 cup of the breadcrumbs in a bowl. Dip each oyster in egg and then in breadcrumbs to coat. Cover the filets with oysters, and then top with the remaining filets.

Beat the other egg. Brush the filets with the beaten egg and sprinkle with the remaining 2 tablespoons of breadcrumbs. Bake at 350°F for 40 minutes.

Serves 4.

Here the author does what he does best: He gets spoon-fed oysters by a pretty lady. I mean, somebody's gotta test all these recipes.

WEST RIVER SCALLOPED OYSTERS

You'll have no trouble getting people to the table with this one. Oysters are great scalloped. It's just a little decadent, like pouring chocolate syrup over chocolate ice cream that is atop a chocolate brownie. You might also call this recipe "Death by Oyster."

1   **pint oysters and liquor**
6   **tablespoons cream**
1   **cup cracker crumbs**
1   **cup dry breadcrumbs plus extra for topping**
1   **stick butter, melted**
   salt and pepper

Drain oysters and reserve liquor. Mix liquor with cream and then add cracker crumbs, breadcrumbs, and melted butter.

In a greased loaf pan, place half the crumb mixture. Then add half the oysters and season with salt and pepper, the rest of the crumbs, and the rest of the oysters. Season again with salt and pepper, and sprinkle with dry breadcrumbs. Bake at 400°F for 20 minutes.

Serves 4.

Before air conditioning, fans were a great way to keep cool and advertise your business at the same time. Most every church, funeral parlor, and seafood market gave fans away. Note this patriotic one. It's a sign of the times.

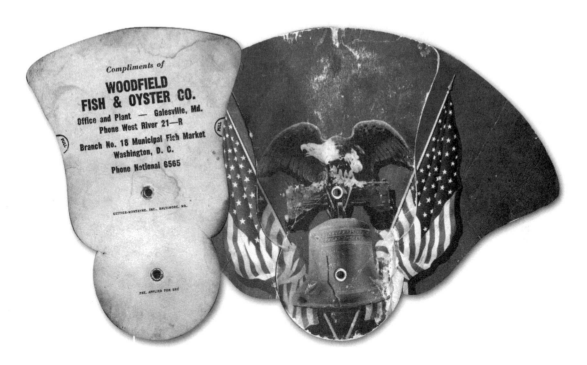

Compliments of
WOODFIELD FISH & OYSTER CO.
Office and Plant — Galesville, Md.
Phone West River 21—R
Branch No. 18 Municipal Fish Market
Washington, D. C.
Phone National 6565

PROTESTANT POINT SAUTÉED OYSTERS

This is a Chesapeake-style sauté with a unique flavor coming from the remarkable fragrance of cumin mixing with garlic and white wine. Talk about a great early autumn dish!

6 tablespoons butter
1 pound medium mushrooms (about 18), sliced
1 quart oysters and liquor
6 small cloves garlic, minced
1½ teaspoons ground cumin
⅔ cup dry white wine

Use 2 large skillets for this quick sauté. Divide the butter between the pans and lightly brown it over medium-high heat, then toss the mushrooms in the browned butter, cooking them until they develop a golden tinge.

Meanwhile, drain the oysters thoroughly in a sieve, put them in a bowl, and coat them well with the garlic and cumin. Add the oysters to the other pan and shake and toss for 3 or 4 minutes or until their edges curl.

When the oysters are cooked, moisten the contents of each pan with the wine, and let the juices bubble up and burn off the wine's alcohol for a minute. Serve immediately with a cold glass of chardonnay.

Serves 6.

Photograph by Vince Lupo.

The author prepares to slurp another dozen at McGarvey's Oyster Bar in downtown Annapolis. Oysters at McGarvey's are often finished off with a glass of the house-brewed specialty: Aviator Draft beer, a reddish-golden brew that goes great with oysters.

SMITHFIELD HANGTOWN FRY

 Tall tales abound from the Gold Rush era, when Placerville was called Hangtown for obvious reasons. According to rumor, this dish was created when a miner struck it rich and demanded the best meal money (or gold) could buy.

- 4 strips bacon
- 1/2 cup Smithfield ham cut into strips
- 6 eggs
- ¼ cup cream
- 2 tablespoons water
- 4 tablespoons chopped fresh parsley
- 3 tablespoons freshly grated Parmigiano-Reggiano cheese
- 1 cup fine dry breadcrumbs
- 1 pint oysters and liquor
- 1 shallot, minced
  chopped fresh parsley
  salt and freshly ground black pepper

In a large ovenproof skillet, sauté the bacon until crisp. Drain on paper towels, crumble, and set aside. Sauté the ham strips in the bacon drippings over medium heat until lightly browned. Drain on paper towels and set aside.

Remove all but 2 tablespoons of the drippings and set the skillet aside.

In a bowl, beat 4 of the eggs until light. Beat in the cream, water, parsley, and Parmigiano-Reggiano cheese. Set aside.

In another bowl, beat the remaining 2 eggs. Spread the breadcrumbs on a plate. Shuck the oysters and discard the shells and oyster liquor. Dip each oyster first in the beaten eggs and then in the breadcrumbs and set aside.

Add the shallot to the drippings in the skillet and cook over medium heat for 1 minute. Add the oysters and cook for one minute on each side. Stir in the bacon and ham. Pour in the egg-cream-parsley mixture and let cook, without stirring, until the eggs begin to set, 4 to 5 minutes. Place the skillet under the broiler until the eggs are golden brown. Sprinkle with parsley and salt and pepper to taste.

Serves 6.

The beautiful old Oyster Catcher, *which you can often see around Spa Creek in Annapolis, was originally built as a skipjack. Later, she was converted into a river cruiser. Today, the* Catcher *has three state-rooms and can be chartered during the spring and fall for private cruises. For information, log onto **www.oystercatchercharters.com**.*

Photograph by Vince Lupo.

SPRING COVE CHICKEN-OYSTER BAKE

The Southern Maryland area (on the Western Shore) has historically been a travel destination for those in search of natural beauty, quiet creeks, and relaxation within a reasonable drive of cities like Washington and Annapolis. Of course, this area's churches are known for their traditional chicken and oyster cookouts. Here's a culinary tip of the hat to those fine institutions.

> 2 **tablespoons all-purpose flour**
> 1 **teaspoon salt**
> ⅛ **teaspoon pepper**
> 1 **3-pound fryer chicken, cut up**
> 1 **tablespoon olive oil**
> ½ **cup chopped onion**
> 3 **cloves garlic, minced**
> 1 **can (15½ ounces) cut green beans, drained**
> 1 **pint oysters and liquor**
> 1 **cup uncooked long-grain rice**
> ½ **cup water**
> 1 **can (8 ounces) tomato sauce**
> 1 **can (6½ ounces) minced clams, drained**

In a plastic bag, combine the flour, salt, and pepper. Shake the chicken, a few pieces at a time, in this mixture to coat. In a large skillet, heat the oil and brown the chicken. Remove the chicken and set aside. Add the onion and garlic to the skillet; cook until tender. Drain the oysters, discarding the liquor, and add them, the green beans, rice, tomato sauce, drained clams, and water. Heat to boiling. Pour into a 13-by-9-by-2-inch baking dish. Arrange the chicken pieces on top. Cover and bake at 350°F for 1 hour.

Serves 6.

This penny postcard, dated Sept. 12, 1905, portrays tongers working the Chesapeake Bay. This was back in the day when men were watermen and oysters were a dime a dozen—if not cheaper.

6685. OYSTER TONGING. *in Chesapeake Bay*

ANGIE'S OSTRICHE ARROSTO

Miss Angie, an old friend of mine, is known for her Italian-style broiled oysters. She loves to get her barbecue grill hot while sipping vodka, telling stories, and loading the grill up with fresh oysters. And when it's too windy to cook this dish out back, she throws them into the broiler. But it's never too windy to sip a little chilled vodka, she says.

> 12   **oysters**
>   **chopped parsley**
> 4   **cloves garlic, chopped**
>   **breadcrumbs**
>   **oregano**
>   **lemon juice**
>   **olive oil**
>   **salt and pepper**

Shuck the oysters, reserving the deep shells and discarding the top shells and liquor. Place the oysters in their shells on a wire rack. Sprinkle the parsley and garlic evenly over them, followed by the breadcrumbs and oregano, and then drizzle with 2 to 3 drops of lemon juice and a little olive oil. Season with salt and pepper and broil for 15 minutes.

Serves 2

Susan's Seafood in New Church, Virginia, is irresistible not only for great fresh-from-the-Bay seafood, but for the many ways you can pay for your selection. I usually just say, while pointing to the guy next to me: "Ahem, put it on his tab."

PUNGOTEAGUE POACHED OYSTERS

The secret to poaching is to cook the food in a liquid that is boiling so slowly that it hardly seems to be boiling at all, with bubbles forming but never quite making it to the surface. Poaching brings out the full, delicate flavor of the oysters and the spices in this dish.

24	oysters in shells
1	bottle (8 ounces) clam juice
1½	tablespoons black peppercorns
4	cloves garlic, roasted
½	teaspoon salt
¼	teaspoon ground allspice
3	tablespoons extra-virgin olive oil
	juice of 1 lime
	lime wedges

Shuck the oysters, reserving the deep shells, discarding the top shells, and pouring the liquor into a small saucepan. Add the oysters, and then add enough clam juice to the pan to just cover the oysters. Remove the oysters and bring the liquid to a boil. Add the oysters back again and reduce the heat to a simmer. Poach the oysters for about 5 minutes, until their edges curl and they begin to plump. With a slotted spoon, remove the oysters immediately, and set them aside. Reserve the poaching liquid.

In a food processor, combine the peppercorns, garlic, salt, and allspice until they form a paste. Add olive oil and lime juice and thin with the poaching liquid. Spoon mixture over the oysters and place in broiler just to bring up the heat. Serve immediately garnished with lime wedges.

Serves 6

Unloading Oysters. Oyster Wharf. Baltimore, Md.

This early 1900s postcard shows the unloading of oysters at the wharf in downtown Baltimore. Today, this same area is home to HarborPlace, Camden Yards, and a revitalized quarter of the city that attracts hundreds of thousands of tourists every year.

Bay Country Oyster and Fish Dish

The Seafood Marketing Authority of Maryland provides this great recipe, which is easily adaptable to different Chesapeake seafood like clams, crab meat, and striped bass (known as rockfish here on the Bay).

- 4   **tablespoons butter**
- 1   **cup finely chopped onion**
- 1   **pound fish fillets, cut into 4 pieces**
- 1   **can (4 ounces) mushrooms**
- ¼   **cup dry sherry**
- ½   **teaspoon salt**
- ⅛   **teaspoon pepper**
- ½   **cup liquid (juice and liquor from mushrooms and oysters)**
- 1   **cup oysters and liquor**

In a large skillet, melt the butter. Add the onions and sauté until glazed, 8 to 10 minutes. Spread the onions evenly over the pan and lay the fish fillets over the top.

Drain the mushrooms, reserving the juice. Spread the mushrooms over the fish. Drain the oysters and reserve the liquor. Mix the sherry, salt, pepper, and mushroom and oyster liquids (½ cup). Pour over the fish. Cover and simmer until the fish flakes easily when tested with a fork, 5 to 8 minutes. Place the oysters in the pan juices around the fish and simmer, uncovered, basting frequently, until their edges curl, about 5 minutes.

Serves 4.

In the early 1900s, Baltimore's Inner Harbor was constantly abuzz with a variety of commercial craft. This view of the oyster fleet from a 1905 postcard makes me think of the oystermen making a good sale and spending most of proceeds on a night out in Charm City. I wish I could have raised a pint with 'em.

Oyster Fleet, Pratt Street, Baltimore, Md.

Pratt Street Casserole

Here is the pinnacle of Chesapeake Bay cooking: Basically, it's a casserole, combining not just oysters but meaty lobsters and lump crab meat. Be sure to have a couple of extra bottles of wine on hand when you serve this dish.

1   **small onion, minced**
⅓   **cup butter**
2   **quarts oysters and liquor**
1   **pound small mushrooms**
⅓   **cup all-purpose flour**
1   **teaspoon salt**
½   **teaspoon nutmeg**
½   **teaspoon paprika**
¼   **teaspoon pepper**
⅛   **teaspoon cayenne pepper**
2   **cups cream**
½   **teaspoon grated lemon rind**
1   **small bay leaf, crumbled**
2   **pounds cooked lobster meat, all shell removed**

1   **pound crabmeat**
1   **green pepper, minced**
½   **cup dry white wine**
2   **egg yolks, beaten**
   buttered breadcrumbs

In a Dutch oven, melt the butter and sauté the onion. Wipe the mushrooms with a damp cloth, quarter them, and add them to the butter. Do not brown! Remove the skillet from the heat, remove the mushrooms and set aside.

Sift the flour, salt, nutmeg, paprika, pepper, and cayenne pepper together. Mix with the cream, lemon rind, and bay leaf. Blend this mixture with the remaining butter in the skillet. Add the lobster meat, crabmeat, green pepper, and reserved mushrooms. Cover and cook on low heat.

Drain the oysters. Bring the oyster liquor to a boil. Add the oysters and cook until their edges curl. Remove the oysters. To the liquor, add the beaten egg yolks and wine, and add to the seafood mixture. Stir well. Add the oysters and mix lightly. Top with buttered breadcrumbs and bake at 375° for 15 minutes.

Serves 12.

Photograph by Vince Lupo.

All in a night's work: Front, seated on left, is Rob McBrayer, and on the right is Ruth McBrayer. I'm standing on the left, and on the right is world-famous New York photographer Bryan Hatchett.

THE INN AT EASTON BARBECUED OYSTERS

This dish comes from Chef Andrew Evans, the culinary maestro behind the Inn at Easton's fantastic menu. Located on Maryland's Eastern Shore, the Inn at Easton is an elegant and classy restaurant. You'll love the chef's smoky rendition.

24	oysters in shells
½	pound sliced smoked bacon
½	cup ketchup
2	tablespoons Worcestershire sauce
2	teaspoons Tabasco sauce
1	tablespoon brown sugar
1	tablespoon lemon juice
	rock salt

Shuck the oysters, reserving the deep shells and discarding the liquor and top shells.

Slice the bacon diagonally into matchstick-size strips. In a sauté pan over medium heat, cook it until halfway done. Drain the fat and set the bacon aside.

To create the barbecue sauce, combine the ketchup, Worcestershire sauce, Tabasco sauce, brown sugar, and lemon juice in a bowl.

Cover a baking sheet with a thin layer of rock salt and place the shells on top. Place an oyster in each shell. Place 4 or 5 strips of bacon on each oyster and then ladle on a tablespoon of sauce.

Broil for 5 minutes, or until the sauce starts to blacken. Serve immediately.

Serves 4.

Just make sure you don't confuse the seafood with the food for the seafood.

OYSTERS AND WILD RICE WICOMICO

Wild rice is known for its luxurious nutty flavor and its chewy texture. Did you know that wild rice isn't really rice at all? Instead, it's a long-grain marsh grass. Despite that, it's delicious, especially when paired with oysters.

1   box (6 ounces) long-grain and wild rice, cooked
1   stick butter, melted
1   quart oysters and liquor
     salt and pepper
     dash of Tabasco sauce
     sprinkle of celery seed
2   cups half-and-half
¼   cup chicken broth
1   medium onion, finely chopped
1   teaspoon thyme
1   tablespoon curry powder
     chopped fresh parsley

Toss the rice and butter until thoroughly mixed. Place half the rice in a 13-by-9-inch baking dish. Drain the oysters, discarding the liquor, and layer them on the rice. Season with salt, pepper, and Tabasco sauce. Top with remaining rice.

In a heavy pan, add the celery seed to the half-and-half and heat; pour in the chicken broth. Stir. Remove the pan from heat and add the remaining ingredients. Pour over the casserole. Bake at 300°F for 45 minutes. Garnish with parsley.

Serves 8.

I don't know what attracted my attention first, the fresh shrimp, the seaside clams or the oysters at $8 a pint. But I do know what keeps me coming back: Yes, I've been trying to buy that spare tire that Tim Taylor keeps on top of his truck.

INDEX

Index

Pies, Soufflés, Quiches, Muffins, Crêpes

Roasted